SHUT UP AND WRITE YOUR FIRST BOOK

GET OVER YOURSELF

48 REASONS THAT STAND IN YOUR WAY

NATASA DENMAN

First published by Ultimate World Publishing 2018
Copyright © 2018 Natasa Denman

ISBN
Paperback - 978-1-922597-10-6
Ebook - 978-1-925830-06-4

Cover design: Ultimate World Publishing
Layout and typesetting: Ultimate World Publishing
Editor: Laura McCluskey

Ultimate World Publishing
Diamond Creek,
Victoria Australia 3089
www.writeabook.com.au

'I've just completed the 48 Hour Author Retreat and I can't praise this retreat enough. It made me focused, it gave me more resources than I thought was humanly possible to have. It's given me structure to how I write my book but more importantly what to do with my book after that. It has given me structure how to implement programs after I'm finished, run workshop and the marketing side has been invaluable.'

Natalie Turvey
Author of *Unbreakable Relationships*

'The retreat experience has been amazing! I loved every minute of it! Everything that I've learned before, during and after this retreat will help me not only to become an author but also grow my business. This weekend I got my book totally finished and I am ready to send it out for editing. During this weekend, I specifically got my 12 chapters done because the unpack was done before that. I've been able to learn so much about multiple ways to leverage my book. This is a blueprint to success for anyone that may find it that don't have a system on how to get their first book out there.'

Kitty Cheng
Author of *Juggling Health and Wealth*

'I could honestly tell you that if I can do this, anyone can do it! From my head, now it's out on paper and I can't wait to actually be able to sell it and help other women who are going through the divorce process. If you're thinking about writing a book, there is no better way than this. I'm a really process-driven individual and to think that I can come away from my busy life and within 48 hours have everything documented, and that I can go back to work on Monday and continue on is just an awesome gift that Natasa & Stuart have provided. Other than that, it is one of good times and you get to meet like-minded people here which has been absolutely amazing. And I think I may just met some friends for life.'

Tanya Somerton
Author of *The Jelly Bean Jar*

'This course and venue has been outstanding for me. Two things that stood out was, changing my book name – that actually challenged me, but we worked through it – the support around it was brilliant. And the other thing that I found extraordinary was being able to have the time to actually do the work, dedicated time to go away and implement the learning on what we needed to do. Fantastic! The support was brilliant and am looking forward to the future.'

James Bernard
Author of *The Bernard Method*

'I just spent this weekend at Natasa Denman's Ultimate 48-Hour Author Weekend Retreat and it was fantastic! I come from the publishing space and I've added marketing to my title because that's my new direction but coming from a publishing background I was trying to find someone who was as good as I was to take over the parts of my business I didn't want to do anymore and meeting my high standards was proving near impossible. I've been searching for someone like Natasa for years and now I've finally found her! If I think she's worth sending all my clients to, you guys better get to one of these events as well! Use Natasa, there's no one as good! If you're thinking about publishing a book, if you are thinking about writing a book, if you're not sure and just wanted someone to talk to about it, Natasa is the girl to go to!'

Kylee Ellis
the Publishing and Marketing Queen

'Ultimate 48-Hour Author is a unique program that has a very methodical system and connections to all the relevant people who support you throughout the authoring process. Most importantly, they have helped many first-time authors already to publish their books. I'm glad I did, and I think Natasa and Moustafa had a big role to play in the publication of my first book. They are awesome!'

Mona AlHebsi, from Dubai
Author of *Beat the Odds*

'For me the Ultimate 48-Hour Author Program is so slick and easy to do. Today people are looking for solutions that are simple to follow. The variety of support provided is endless, like having Natasa and Stuart astounding knowledge on tap, your publisher is sorted out for you, an editor is selected for you and then of course Richard who transcribes your book, Kevin who does a photographic shoot with you and Nikola who can help you with your diagrams, book cover, etc. Oh my word, the support is amazing. There is even more... you can attend Unlimited 2-Day Face-to-Face Masterclasses (which run four times a year) to support you with marketing your book. The Ultimate 48-Hour Author Program has your back at all times. Natasa and her team want to see you succeed and the assistance is immeasurable.'

Karen Singery
Author of *After the Shock*

'I met Natasa in the spring at a half day workshop in Phoenix. I decided I want to jump right in and do my book. So I came to Australia and I made the trip a vacation. When you're coming this far, you may as well stay for two weeks. The retreat is fabulous, they take care of everything, and you don't have to worry about anything but your book and recording it. They guide us to every step, through media, photography, covers, everything, editing. We got to meet the whole team, Natasa and Stuart are the head of the team. I've made wonderful friends from all over Australia. You must jump in if you want to write a book! This is the time to do it!'

Bridget Dwyer
Author of *The Abundant Teacher*

DEDICATION

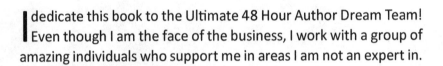

I dedicate this book to the Ultimate 48 Hour Author Dream Team! Even though I am the face of the business, I work with a group of amazing individuals who support me in areas I am not an expert in.

Huge shout-out to our Ultimate 48 Hour Authors who put their trust in us helping them birth their first books. Thank you so much for being brave and always stepping up in supporting our mission!

CONTENTS

INTRODUCTION

The best time to start something is when you're not ready. When was the last time you were truly ready to take a leap of faith in your life? Whether it was to change your career, starting something new, make a big decision to invest in property, or buy something that was going to impact your life significantly? I bet if you look back in all of those situations the timing was not ideal, or far from perfect.

Writing a book is exactly that; a leap of faith that we are never actually ready to take. However, there comes a point in our lives when the reasons why we should do it seriously outweigh the reasons why we shouldn't. For the past five years I have travelled all over the world helping people write their first books. I've been exposed to many cultures from countries such as the USA, Australia (which is my home country), New Zealand, and Middle Eastern counties (primarily the UAE). I've had clients from Germany, Syria, Saudi Arabia, Qatar, Russia, and many more. Through all of these cultures the same patterns come up as to why people don't take that leap of faith to write their first book.

I want this to be a conversation between you and me. I want this book to be utilised to flick across to any of the 48 reasons as to why people don't say yes to themselves, and actually write that very first book. If it was me, I'd read the biggest challenges I have currently when I think about writing my first book.

Writing the very first book is always going to be the most awkward and unfamiliar journey. For those people who do know me or have been to some of my events, they know that my mum's biggest piece of wisdom is, 'Every beginning is hard .' She has told me this since I was young, and every time I start something new I hear her words ringing through my head.

To you, my dear first-time author, I will say the same thing: *every beginning is hard, unfamiliar, or awkward.* After you've done it once, you'll know that everything that you thought about yourself, this process, and about what it means to become an author was actually not true. Then you will come to a place where writing books is addictive to the point that you want to write book after book after book, and you just need to figure out how to find the time, resources, and what would be the next best steps to do exactly that.

This book was written for those who have never written a book before. It covers the challenges, obstacles and thoughts that people have when they're embarking on this journey for the very first time. I'm writing it because I wrote a book called *Ultimate 48 Hour Author* and, to date, we have helped more than 300 people become first-time published authors.

The problems, challenges and issues that I continually bump against when I meet those first-time authors are the difference between someone saying yes on this journey to themselves, and completely ruling themselves out of it. I'll be covering a majority of mind-set issues and roadblocks that people have around making this decision which is the biggest obstacle to overcome. I'll also discuss the publishing industry, legalities, copyright, and other things that can prevent people from moving to those next steps.

I'm writing this book, because I'm very serious about hitting my big vision and goal of helping more 1,000 people become first-time published authors. That is my next milestone, so I really want more people to see that there's actually nothing to worry about. At the other end of this there will be a massive transformation, on a personal or a business level.

How can you use this book? You can read it cover to cover, but you're probably not going to have all 48 obstacles that I discuss in this book; I am hoping you don't! Jump across to the ones that are the hot points for yourself, and then return to some of the others later. It's really interesting to understand what other people may be thinking and worrying about when it comes to writing their first book.

To add even more value in this book, I have included interviews with some of my Ultimate 48-Hour Authors. These authors have a variety of styles, books, and intentions when it comes to writing. I also looked at a variety of challenges they had when embarking on their journey to becoming a first-time author. So many authors wanted to share their stories that it was really hard to choose what would go in the book. Even though I did not include every single interview, I have compiled the rest in a downloadable PDF you can access by going here:

http://bit.ly/shutupfreeebook

I wrote my very first book in 2011. It is the thing that got my business off the ground; it turned from a business that had two paying clients to a fully-booked weight-loss coaching practice.

The idea of Ultimate 48-Hour Author was developed and executed first in 2013. To date we have run 21 retreats, and have put almost 300 people through this program.

Last year I took the business global. I'm really excited to share these insights with you, because they are a collection of more than 150 half-day events that I have run to introduce people to the concept and help them write their very first book. Throughout these events, it is unfortunate that I have observed and seen so many people say no to themselves and not feeling worthy of this process, and what it takes to become an author.

I want you to be different. I want you to understand what your mind is trying to tell you, and how to move past the feelings of unworthiness, fear, and lack of understanding of the process.

Let's get started!

PART 1

Your Mental Blocks

1. BUILD YOUR WORTH

Searching on the Internet for a few popular definitions of self-worth lead me to understand that it is the opinion you have about yourself and the value you place on yourself.

You might think you are a good person who deserves good things, or you believe that you are a bad person who deserves bad things. One of the biggest obstacles that people encounter when wanting to write their first book is the ability to value themselves to a point that they are able to take that leap of faith in this journey.

Self-worth is you saying, 'I'm worthy of this journey. I'm worthy to invest in myself, to grow, to evolve, and to be that next-level individual who has transformed from a caterpillar to a butterfly.

Your self-worth can take a huge hit growing up, depending on your upbringing. It could be a false belief about yourself that was actually not manifested or created by you. It could also be something someone told you or said to you that you still believe is true.

I want to share three quick ways to improve your self-worth that may be able to help in other areas in your life, not just when writing a book:

1. To develop increased self-worth towards knowing and believing that you deserve good things in life, start spending money on things that you love. Spend money on good quality things; things that you know you're worthy of having for yourself.

2. Start setting aside time for yourself where you can indulge in whatever activity gives you joy, whether it's

reading or going for a massage. Do something for yourself that is, in a way, selfish and putting you in line first.

3. Start saying no to people. If you're one of those people who is always a yes person, one thing to understand is that successful people say no a lot more frequently than they say yes. Learn how to say no. You'll be showing that you value your time and the people that you choose to hang around with, and the way you choose to spend your own time and money.

4. Self-worth is one that is really going to be the make or break for your decision to write your first book. Overcome this and the rest becomes history!

2. BUST YOUR FEAR

The number one reason why people don't write their first books is self-doubt, or fear. The only two fears we are born with are the fear of falling, and the fear of loud sounds.

The fear of not being good enough is one of three core fears we learn to have as human beings; the others are the fear of not being loved, and the fear of not belonging. The fear of not being good enough is something that is embedded in our minds in the very early stages of our life, the imprint period of 0-7 years old. But it's not real; it's something that we exaggerate in our minds, making a mountain out of a molehill. By giving into this, we are actually honouring the naysayers. We are, in a way, proving to ourselves that we truly are not good enough, and those who told us that when we were children must be right.

Overcome the fear of self-doubt and really bust through it, like in Susan Jeffers' famously-named book Feel the Fear and Do It Anyway.

This is the best advice that I can share. Go and read her book as it will give you awesome strategies. If nothing else, answer this question for yourself: what is the worst thing that could happen? Often, it's never as bad as what our mind tends to make it out to be. You cannot escape fear, sometimes you cannot even minimise it, but you can learn to live with fear and deal with it regardless.

I heard one of my authors, Rachael Sheldrick (check out her interview at the back of the book) say at an event that, 'Sick means go .' She meant that when you get that sick feeling in your tummy when you're so scared that you're not good enough, or maybe you cannot figure out how you're going to make this happen for yourself financially, or time-wise, skills-wise, etc., that feeling of sickness is actually an indicator that you must move to that next step. Say yes, and then work out the how. On the other side of that lies the transformation and evolution of you as a person to the next level.

With more than 300 people having been on this journey with me, I've never, ever had anyone come up to me and say, 'Nat, I wish I didn't do this .' They've never told me of horrible backlash, criticism, or estrangement from family and friends. Everyone to this date always says, 'I'm so glad you made me do it.'

3. FIND THE TIME

If you really want to do something you will find a way. If you don't, you'll find an excuse. This was famously said by Jim Rohn, and this is one that I talk to my first-time authors about because, realistically, that excuse almost every time is either going to be lack of time or money.

Time comes up more than money, and is the second most common reason why people won't write their first book. It's one of those things that ends up being pushed down the list of priorities. You keep pushing it down that list and not being resourceful enough to do it in the fastest time possible. The time excuse usually is a hiding place to conceal the mindset of fear-based thoughts.

The whole reason behind me bringing out the Ultimate 48-Hour Author system to the marketplace is because as we get busier and busier in our days, it becomes more of a challenge to write a book the old-fashioned way. It's challenging to set aside that time (sometimes people can take months and years to do this) and actually do it in a very focused and systematic way when you don't know how.

The time excuse has been busted for you guys. My system is out there – read *Ultimate 48-Hour Author* and you will learn how. A book can be executed in just five hours, such as the one you're reading right now. In less than 24 hours I spoke out the full contents of this book. It was then sent through to my transcriptionist who typed what I said, and four days later the cleaned up transcripts were compiled into a manuscript, and forwarded onto the editor early the following week. A total of 10 days to turn it all around, and put into the experts' hands who will do the rest.

It can be as simple as that.

No longer should time be an excuse. If there are other reasons around time, which certainly can be valid, we're going to address those in later chapters. Again, as Jim Rohn said, 'If you really want to do something you will find a way. If you don't you will find an excuse.' Not only this, but you'll talk yourself out of it.

Time is relative in terms of what you believe about it. Successful people actually never say they don't have enough time. They may seem like they are busy individuals, but they are abundant

6

with time because they know where to prioritise it and where to say to no.

Writing a book is not a time-waster but a time-saver in the future. People I meet tell me all the time that they are continuously repeating themselves to clients and others. This is exhausting. Write your book and then refer others to it before speaking with them one-on-one. I save so much time documenting everything I do in my books, videos, and systems. Do it once and you can share and sell it forever – no brainer!

4. MAKE THE GAP – FIND THE MONEY

The process of self-publishing your book is not one that is affordable. After all, think about the types of experts that you need to make a book look and sound great: the editors, layout, designers, printers, etc. The Ultimate 48-Hour Author program takes it up to another level because we offer the full project management, suppliers, the mentorship, and all of the support that surrounds the marketing and the leveraging of that book. Money is one that I find is a significant obstacle for people.

A lady I met on my travels said, when discussing her writing a book, 'Look, Nat, whenever in life I have made a financial gap I had no idea how I was going to fill it.'

When we talk about a 'gap', it's about investing in something that you didn't anticipate that you were going to be investing in: for example, finding the funds when wanting to upgrade your home or put an extra staff member on your team in your business. This ends up creating a massive extra expense that needs to be maintained long term. That can be scary.

But I know from observing this in other people's lives that every time they make a gap within their financial standpoint they figure out how to fill that gap. What ends up happening is there's this pressure that ends up coming into our lives. This pressure creates the conditions and gives birth to this ability for us to become more resourceful.

The simplest way I can explain this is by looking at the journey of having my three children. Often people say, 'Oh, children make you poor. Before children I was so rich.' I actually choose to believe the complete opposite. Since having children I've become richer and richer, and more abundant financially because I feel like I have this rocket up my bum to perform, to be able to feed my family and put a roof over their heads.

This is also the same ability I needed to tap into to help my husband quit his day job and join the business that we now have been running together for six years, fending for ourselves. In the last six months my mum joined the business, as well. I was able to give her the gift of semi-retirement, and she gives us a little bit of help around the business and with the children so we can continue to thrive and help more and more people when travelling.

I kept creating those gaps in my life, and I know this is the same situation when trying to write a book. You will end up creating a gap, especially if you are going down the route of self-publishing, which is most of the time what first-time authors will do. Your brain will figure out a way of how to manifest, or how to bring in or get some extra work to fill that gap, and to see you come out more abundant the other end.

I believe we all are very resourceful people, but when there is no pressure on our current situation we choose to simply plateau. When we put a little bit of pressure on and push ourselves to that next level, we choose and make decisions accordingly so that we can continue swimming, versus sinking. I think this is a very big, important lesson that I've had to learn over the last eight years in business.

Every time I've had to invest in experts who were going to take my business and life to the next level (so long as I followed the steps of what they said to me and the way they mentored me) I've always got 10-20 times return on investment, if not more so, as I continue implementing the things that I have learnt from them as the years roll by.

Money should never be an issue; it's only when you have been known to waste money in the past without following through on the instructions that you should be worried about. If your reference is that you follow through every time you have invested in someone, however, then the answer is very simple; just go for it and get it done, because if you follow the recipe, there is no doubt you're going to get a result at the other end.

Remember, rules are meant to be followed, not broken.

5. BREAK THE PERFECTIONISM CYCLE

'Perfectionism equals insanity and looping.' This was the lesson that I learnt at my NLP training seven years ago from a gorgeous mentor of mine, Alice Haemmerle. When she said that it really made me think. It made a lot of sense. It was one of those penny-drop moments. Time and time again in my workshops I meet countless perfectionists who actually pride themselves on this. When I talk a little bit more about the topic I actually say, 'Look, guys, the secret to success on your authoring journey is not about perfectionism, it's about progress. If I was worried about being super perfect with how everything came out, or every tiny little error that I made in the things that I put out there in the world, then they would have never gone out, and I would have taken twice as long to get to the point where I am today.'

Sitting here eight years, and eight books later, with the thousands of clients and people who I've touched across the world ... none of this happened because I did things perfectly. It happened because I was real and authentic. Often when people do read my books they'll find an error here and there, and so-fricking-what? I'll tell you a secret; those are left there for the anal people. They're there for the clients who I actually don't want to work with. I carefully select people who pass our 'no dickheads' policy, because in life we are not perfect. As human beings we were created imperfect. We are meant to learn from those things so that when we stuff up we get to grow to the next level. This gift of imperfection helps us grow and evolve and become a better person.

Perfectionism is something that is going to prevent you from writing your first book, and if you pride yourself on being one maybe it's time to shift this belief. Make a decision that you'll do the best you can with what you know right now, and if you don't, laugh it off, take the lesson, and do it better the next time around.

Please remember that perfectionism is looping and insanity, and it's not going to serve you to write your first book. You wouldn't believe the amount of times I've heard people who talk to me about writing their books, and the fact that their book has been in their computer for 5-10 years. I say to them, 'You've got to start again, that content is actually irrelevant now. You've probably grown so much, you know so much more after all these years that have passed.'

This is the whole reason why I write a book a year, because I learn so much and then reverse-engineer those learnings so I can help others, who are then going to follow in my footsteps in terms of wanting to model what we have created. It is your time now to *focus on progress over perfectionism.*

6. STOP MOVING AROUND DECK CHAIRS

My husband and I came up with this little saying when we meet people who have been writing their book for 5-10 years and still haven't finished it. It's interesting when people hear about what I do and specialise in, they say, 'Oh, I'm writing my book.' Then I say to them, 'Oh wonderful, tell me what it's all about, when is it going to be out? Have you published it?' And their next comment is, 'Oh yes, well I've been doing it for about 5-10 years and it's getting there', and all those other excuses. Then I say, 'Oh, so you've been moving around deck chairs?' Then we have a little laugh about it.

This extends upon the perfectionism pattern, and I really wanted to single out this challenge so many get stuck in. Moving around deck chairs is going to get you nowhere. Stop reshuffling things in your manuscript, and whatever else you're fluffing around with that is preventing you from actually getting the results out of your book and doing the exciting things that come beyond publishing that book – the marketing, the promotion, the growth of your credibility and your profile, and your personal development. Just consider all the wonderful opportunities that you're missing out on because you continue to move deck chairs around.

Choose today to set that deck chair in one spot and let it be, because the point of the matter is once you've written your very first book, the next step is to think about your next one; to figure out other ways you can help people, because what happens as you grow your intellectual property is you sell a whole lot more of it. As people buy one and then enjoy it, all of a sudden they want the others, too. I have firsthand experience in this. Nowadays, I'm selling $90-$150 worth of products per person at my events, which means that passive income is really coming in a lot more without having to sell my time for money.

You might think, 'I just want to write my first book right now', but I can guarantee you it does become addictive, something you want to continue working on. It is very therapeutic and really rewarding hearing feedback from others about your book. Set up that deck and move off it, and get onto the next deck so you can coordinate and set up so more people can benefit from the shortcuts or the strategies of the story or system that you're wanting to write about.

7. IMMORTAL LEGACY

I recently read a book by Mark Manson, *The Subtle Art of Not Giving a Fuck*. I loved how he talked about legacy. Most of us do want to write our book because we want to leave some kind of a legacy and make a difference in the world. He says, 'Do you know the real reason why people want to write their book? Because they treat it as their immortality project.' This really stood out to me; I had never considered it like that. We'd all like to think that we're going to live on in some way beyond our physical presence here; that our wisdom, our philosophy for life, or whatever else we want to impart with the world about our career or what we are an expert in, so it's really wonderful to know that it can become immortal if put in a book.

One thing I know for sure is that your family isn't going to throw out that book if you wrote it. It's most likely going to be passed on from generation to generation and spoken about: 'Hey, you know your great-grandma wrote this book?' After all, people don't throw out books, and leaving a legacy is really you imparting something from within you that can help those future generations.

Generations do evolve, and things are done differently at different times, but we all know of famous books like *Think and Grow Rich* and *The Alchemist* that have been around for decades, if not close to a century. How much timeless wisdom is shared throughout them? If you're writing a book that's autobiographical, or a story about your life and the lessons that you've learnt, that's another way to share your perspective and leave your legacy.

I can see my little kids who, at the time of writing this book are three, six, and nine, starting to take interest and having a look at my books, and I know that this is going to be a major part of their education and what they will know of me and about me. I have chosen to fully step out and share my thoughts, beliefs, the strategies that I have learnt from running a small business from home while creating a lifestyle most can only dream of. I'm trusting that some of that will be passed onto them, so they can model and have that future for themselves in a most positive way where they feel empowered. Ultimately, I'm grateful for the way my mum raised me and the lessons that she imparted on me. Your book will have that impact on your family, too —don't deny them this gift.

If you're not a parent then it doesn't matter, because you'll be impacting other people's lives who have encountered the same challenges, problems, or obstacles that you'll be covering as you write your book.

Leave that legacy; don't die with the music still within you. These were beautiful words shared by one of my workshop participants a couple of years ago in Melbourne. I wonder if he ever wrote his book ...

8. BEYOND CRITICISM

All the way through life we get criticised at some point. Writing a book is no different, and getting criticism is a good thing because it means that you have shared your message, and you're either triggering people who really need your help, or you're triggering those who wish they did what you have just done.

Criticism is one thing that should be embraced because if we're not making a disruption then we're playing it too safe, walking on eggshells around people. To be truly honest, in my journey of writing a book and seeing so many people become first-time authors, I've heard a teeny-tiny amount of bad feedback.

98% of the time I hear so much positive encouragement that trumps any criticism that may have been dished out. When you have one person criticise you, and 100 others encourage you and say how awesome what you are doing is, you're not really going to be affected by that one person.

It's usually weighed that way, especially for the first time writing a book; most of the time they will be pleasantly surprised, rather than thinking, 'Oh who the hell does he/she think she is?' Yes, people may think that, but so what? When you have gone through this process, you will end up having a much thicker skin, meaning that criticism is not going to be very much on your radar, or something that's really going to disturb you. I have found that hearing criticism of what I do just doesn't affect me anymore, because I know I've done the right thing with integrity, I've shared everything I wanted to share, and I have always acted with honesty and given people what I have promised.

I'm famous for saying, 'If you can put your head on the pillow at night and know deep down that you have helped as many people with integrity, honesty, and with everything you've promised, and you've responded to all your messages, then you have nothing to worry about.' People cannot be in your life; people are only observing from the outside, so they cannot see the full depth behind what is truly going on. Those who criticise are doing it from a superficial judgement and have not taken the time to get to know you or what you do properly.

They can judge certainly on experiences, on the way you come across in your videos, or whatever it is that you deliver in the content of your message, however, they can never go on that internal part of you that knows that what you're doing has been done with wanting to help others. As long as that is the case, then criticism is something that you can put to the side and just go forward and help people.

9. GARAGE FULL OF BOOKS

The common thing I hear from people when I meet them is, 'I'm so worried that I'm going to end up with a garage full of books.' I think that's a fear that has been embedded in people's minds, or perhaps might be true for many authors and that's why it's a common saying. The reality is that if you follow everything we teach you on how to market and leverage your book, there's nothing to worry about when it comes to selling the units of books that you choose to get at the beginning of your package. Certainly, our intention is that you keep reprinting your book time and time again.

With the onset of print-on-demand options nowadays, you don't really need to start with a ton of books, thousands of books that end up cluttering your garage. You can choose to print 500 to begin with. That's what we begin our authors with in our program, and personally I just do 100 at a time. Once I sell out of those, I order my next 100 through the print-on-demand facility. That way I'm never overwhelmed by having a ton of books in the garage.

In reality, the fear behind having a garage full of books is that people are not being clear on how they are going to market and sell those units. There are so many different ways to sell books – people have even written books on how to sell books. A garage full of books is just an old saying, perhaps from a time when books were being printed in droves. Authors who don't put in effort into their marketing are guaranteed to have them sitting at home for a long time.

One thing I'd like to advise you about marketing your first book is that it is really important that you learn how to do it properly for yourself. Please don't outsource this part of the process to other people because once you know how to do it, then in future you can get others to execute this for you. Because you are your book, people engage with the author and you have a higher chance of selling a lot more books, especially for your first one. Always stand beside your book, get your hands dirty, get out there and pound the pavement, turn up at places, do some book launches, post on social media, add value to people, and you will never get stuck with a garage full of books.

In fact, you will be ordering and reordering so you can use your book as the most powerful business card on steroids you could have.

10. SUCCESS IS THE PROBLEM

When I address the point of fear with people around writing their first book, they often say they have a fear of failure. I correct them then, saying, 'It is actually your fear of success that is preventing you from writing your first book.' They look at me with a puzzled expression on their face, and I explain further. On a subconscious level, we humans, at some point in time, have observed success to mean something different. When we observe successful people, we think they're busy and that we wouldn't want to live life like that. I have actually had those comments posted on my social media platforms when I share about my life and my passion, it does look like I have a busy life, however, it's not like that.

When it comes to building a business whatever success that you're after, it may be busy as you're getting things off the ground. In this particular case we're talking about becoming well-known because of your book, and the credibility that you'll be building out there. Once they hear my story and the things that are required to write that book and leverage it, they may think that it means I will get successful. They think, 'I will get too busy', which equals, 'I will have no life.'

As human beings we work so hard and we strive to achieve some level of lifestyle and work/life balance within our daily lives and the experiences we end up having. Fear of success comes from the subconscious belief that you're going to get busy and, therefore, you won't have a life. As a result you sabotage yourself each time you try. By keeping yourself small you get to say safe without creating havoc and chaos in your life.

After speaking to many people over the years, I continuously hear comments like, 'I couldn't do what you do', or, 'I couldn't do what a certain celebrity or another successful person is doing. It just seems like they're always on.' I'll tell you from this side of the fence, having gone through a fairly busy first 2-3 years to get the business off the ground and to reach that tipping point towards ease and winning back time in my life, we can now take four months off every year to travel with our kids, to have quality time with one another. We have been doing this for the past five years.

Our business is intense for five and a half months a year. We do two massive national tours of events per year. We have also gone international the last couple of years, but we're pulling back from that kind of travel moving forward as we know we want to stay in Australia where we have the biggest impact. International clients can work with us remotely.

We've have got our evenings back. We don't work Friday, Saturday, and Sunday, so I have three-day long weekends because the business is systemised and set up to a point that it's leveraged, and doesn't need me so much. We can take that time off and, realistically, we do need that time because we have intense periods where we're working very hard, and very long hours. Then we have intense periods of rest and rejuvenation, so we can come back stronger and fresher once again to take our business and life to the next level.

Fear of success is one that is a lot bigger than fear of failure, so watch out what you believe about success on a subconscious level and look to change those beliefs if you find yourself sabotaging this. Success actually means more time, ease, and quality of activities and memories that you can build with your loved ones.

11. WATCH OUT! RESISTANCE AHEAD

One of the biggest things that I see happen to authors, even after they have taken the leap and decided to write their very first book, is resistance!

The first time I see it is as our half-day workshop approaches. This is where I normally meet my future first-time authors to-be for the very first time.

Around 20% of people who are registered and have paid for this workshop don't show up. Just before, during, or after the event I get messages and emails that certain things have arisen in their life out of nowhere. They have come down with an illness, a car accident has happened, a child has had to stay home, all these little road blocks keep manifesting in front of them as they were about to embark on this new journey of writing their first book. It's very interesting and I often congratulate the people in the room on actually making it to the event. We tend to manifest resistance in our path when we're about to embark on a transformation. For our little critter brain, this can mean life or death. In this case, writing a book would mean death to it, therefore manifesting resistance to avoid the change. It's like that prehistoric side comes gets activated. Even though someone has paid for the process, the stories keep coming.

Where I see this start to come up once again is one month before our retreat. As time gets closer, more and more things happen for people. There have been deaths in the family, accidents, house moves, business shifts, employees leaving, colds, missed flights, and flights being cancelled. So many things standing in people's way to progress in writing their book, so at one month before the retreat I send them a 30-minute mindset webinar that I've recorded called 'The Top 7 Mindset Challenges That Come Up in the Last Month.'

The feedback when I share it is always, 'Wow, Nat, how did you know this was happening to me?' Having been through 21 retreats now, and reaching almost 300 people, the patterns repeat themselves. We are not too dissimilar to one another. The things that we manifest, especially when it comes to writing a book, is the universe testing you and asking the question, 'Are you worthy of your success?'

Watch out for resistance along this journey, because it will pop its head up when you least want or expect it. Just keep pushing through, deal with the obstacles as they arise. Keep putting one foot in front of the other, and before you know it the next time you go on this journey and you're writing book two, three, four, there will be none of that because you will have dealt with that part of yourself that was so fearful and scared of this journey. You will see that it becomes easy and effortless every time thereafter.

12. YOU ARE SPECIAL

When I meet people and share the success stories of people we have helped to become first-time authors, I have quite a few attendees at my events say, 'I don't think I'm as special as those people. You must have to be a certain type of personality, or have certain level of resources or traits to really do this.' I think that's complete BS. When I decided to write my first book, I didn't think that I was anything special. I just thought you opened up your computer and started writing. I knew that I would be up for a lot of writing, of course, because a book is a significant number of words that have to be written over a specific amount of time. For me, the first book took about 80 days. I set aside a couple of hours a week, and my goal was to write seven pages in each week. I was aiming for 90 Word pages over 90 days.

How I framed it to myself was basically, 'Who can't write a page a day?' I progressed in completing seven pages in two, two-hour writing sessions, pretending as if they were a paying client. Whether it was flowing or not flowing, I was sitting down and writing my book.

It's really key to understand that people who become authors are no different from you and me. They basically just had a passion, an idea, a story, or an expertise they wanted to share, and they developed the discipline and the consistency in pulling this jigsaw puzzle together to complete that book.

Please understand that you don't need to be anything special. Everyone who has a desire to write a book can write one, and once you know how to write one you can write an unlimited number of books. One thing I thought after I finished my very first book is that I felt like I had emptied my whole head into this book, and there was absolutely nothing left.

As time went on and I became better and better at developing content, and I grew and experienced more in my life and business, I started to structure that content in the way that I now teach people to structure their books. I just needed to think about the thing that I wanted to write, and then reverse-engineer the process of how I would show someone to do that specific process or system.

As long as there's a desire, you don't need to be anything special. If you're following a process and a structure, and are given the tools and the resources to be able to do it (like the team that's going to help you pull it all together) then there's no doubt you will become a published author. Back yourself! You are special.

13. CURE TO PROCRASTINATION

Do you want to know the cure to procrastination? I once wrote a full program that covered the 10 keys to busting procrastination, but nowadays I believe it boils down to one key thing: *the cure to procrastination is to make a commitment to someone else.* In life we don't have a lot of accountability for the things we want to achieve, and this is why it is always recommended to have coaches and mentors on our journey. Whether we want to improve our life in a certain area, or we want to grow a successful business, procrastination is no different. This is why I believe writing your very first book and investing with someone who will hold you accountable, show you the ropes, and has all the systems in place to help you go from start to finish is really what's going to nip procrastination in the bud.

I'm constantly launching new programs or products. About four years ago I developed my own planner. Every year for the last four years I brought out the following year's planner. In order for me not to procrastinate in creating this product, I went into my inner circle where people already liked me, trusted me, and knew me, and I announced to them that I was going to do this. At the same time, I created a PayPal button, a way to be paid for the pre-sales of this particular planner, and I offered it $20 cheaper than it would be when it was released to get support and commitment from people. Of course, those people who had loved my books and worked with me before thought it was a great idea and supported my new idea of bringing out this planner.

I ended up selling around 20-30 planners at that time, which wasn't a significant number, however, it was big enough to pay for part of my printing, as well as the full internal design of this product that was going to come out in the next 2-3 months. Of course, what happened then was I got to work. I had to follow through with my graphic design, I had to source out printers, and I had to get it delivered when I had promised to my pre-purchasers. This is really more about the commitment I made to other people. Understanding that these people had paid me for a product that didn't exist put the pressure on me to deliver the goods.

The concept behind procrastination and really eliminating it from your life is to *sell something first and then build it*. As long as you have got the ability to communicate what that thing is and the benefits behind it, people who obviously are warm in your network will end up supporting you, and then the next step is to follow through. You don't want to let people down, and you'll end up looking an idiot who cannot be trusted.

The cure to procrastination is to make a commitment to someone else!

22

14. YOU ARE UNIQUE

A big question that is raised at my half-day event around writing a book in 48 hours is when people's ideas have similar genres to ones that already exist in the marketplace. They say, 'How am I any different?' This is one of my favourite objections, because I was in a similar place when I chose to write my very first book, *The 7 Ultimate Secrets to Weight Loss*. By writing that first book, I was entering an arena where there were thousands upon thousands of weight loss books in the niche.

The one thing that I knew from the get-go is that no one is me, no one has my DNA, and no one has my way of thinking, my flavour. Therefore, my book will be different because I will be the one standing next to it, promoting it, connecting with people, and building my brand with it.

I always say to people to truly to embrace that – the fact that no one can take the you out of your business; the way you deliver the information, with your stories, with your experiences, and with your insights that you have had on this journey is what makes your story or system unique.

Your book may not be a system. It might be a story, and that makes it even more unique. This objection is more relevant to those people who are writing a book in a genre or a niche that has been done many times over.

An example of such a niche or genre is personal development. So many people have written books on personal development, how to be more empowered, how to live the best life, and all that kind of stuff. But it doesn't matter, even if you come from this particular angle, the difference is you. Don't rule it out just because someone else may have written on this topic. At the end of the day you're the one who needs to be out there with your book. You're the one who needs to promote it, and you're the one who's going to be meeting people.

Ultimately, the way that you're going to build the fame around your book or your message is going to start from you sharing information, being active on online platforms, going out networking, meeting people, and really having it beside you and letting it introduce you as that credible expert.

The ultimate goal is for you to be helping people beyond your book. It's not just about your book; it will be more about what else can you do for people now that they have read this awesome information that you have shared. It will be about how they can further engage you, because it is then with the implementation that you will see a transformation in your ideal clients. Just like when I share my system where you're reading this book, or you may have read *Ultimate 48 Hour Author.* Many people will do that and still do nothing about actually becoming first-time authors.

In reality, for those that do take the leap and join us at the full program where we offer everything from start to finish for them, it is there that we implement, that we handhold, that we have accountability, that we have a family-like community, support and all of the resources and suppliers that we need to make it a reality. It is there that we get that true transformation.

Don't do a disservice to people by just offering a book. What else can they do with you that is going to make a big difference in their lives in terms of how you're solving a particular problem in your niche?

15. STOP BEING SELFISH

In my half-day event I ask this question: 'If you don't do something about writing a book, what will happen?' One of the answers that comes up is that people will miss out on the awesome information and the shortcuts and lessons that I have to share. I say, 'Look, let's just summarise that in one word – selfish.'

You get to be selfish. I say, 'Who are you to decide and hold back on the gold, the wisdom, and the information that you have spent so many years dissecting, distilling and making better, so others could benefit, and so they don't have to go through the pain of making all the mistakes and the failures that you've been through to get to where you are today?'

Stop being selfish! Give the world that wisdom and the gold that you've got to share. If anything, the people who will firstly benefit from this are your nearest family and friends, and after that the ripple will spread. I always say to people who do want to make a huge, global difference that the difference needs to start from your own household. You're then going to make a difference within a 10-15km radius from your home in your local community. It then spreads to your whole city, then your state (if you live in a state), then your country, and finally the world.

I can honestly, hand on heart say that this is the exact process I've been through in the last eight years. In my first couple of years, I was just working with my community and impacting my life, and changing the way I thought. This was transforming my family in a completely different way. Our beliefs and thinking was shifting in a new direction.

Don't be selfish because there's always someone out there looking for what you've got to offer. When you meet that person you know you can help 100%, and that you will be able to serve. I know that every single person, if they knew that they could help someone else, would do it because we come from a giving spirit and have the desire deep down to make a difference in other people's lives.

Stop being selfish, write that first book, and impact the people you're meant to reaching with your message today!

16. BE THE MOTHER DUCK

If you have ever observed nature, you would see that as the mother duck leads and her baby ducklings walk behind her. They walk and walk and walk, and it is only when the mother chooses to change direction that the ducklings straighten up and follow behind her.

Joe Pane shared this in one of the speaking engagements that I got to see him deliver a couple years ago. There's a saying that people's ducks need to line up before they can write their first book. This is a very common one: 'I'll write my book when I finish this, I'll write my book when I get more clients, I'll write my book when I have more experience and more expertise, I'll write my book when I have finished my studies, I'll write my book once I have found the money.'

We started off this book to say that the best time to do something is when you're not ready, and that your ducks will line up when you decide to turn left or right – the turn towards making the decision of writing your first book.

Often it is the writing of the book that keeps getting pushed down on the list of priorities, because other ducks need to line up before that is the major priority and the very next thing to do. In reality, as human beings, we know our ducks are never going to line up. It is us who drives this bus that decides where it's going to turn and what it's going to do. We don't know what's around that corner.

You don't have the benefit of hindsight to know that now is the right time to write your first book, but I can tell you that having gone through this myself and my clients, I have the benefit of hindsight to know that every time each and every one of those people, including myself, did say yes on the journey, those ducks did line up and other things sorted themselves out; they were able to fill the gap, find the money, figure out where they were going to find the time. Once you commit to a process it becomes real and it's really starts to play out.

That is why I believe writing your first book should always be with someone who has done it before, who has walked that path, who's got the experience and the insights on the challenges and obstacles that they understand you are going face.

Every time there is fear there is resistance, there is criticism that may arise, perfectionism patterns, I can call my clients on it. I know exactly what is going on and what game they are trying to play. Your mind will play games with you, and you will buy into what it's saying, but it is the external person, who is mentoring and coaching you through this journey, whose job it is to see this, and with experience will be easily able to read your patterns and call you on it.

Allow someone to be that for you, because we cannot trust ourselves. Our subconscious mind is always trying to keep us alive and safe. Remember, this is only a prehistoric version of staying part of a tribe. Writing a book will make you stand out and be different – just know your tribe will follow when you back yourself and do this in time. They always do! Just read the interviews in this book and see what has happened after the fact.

17. DREAM STEALERS

Whenever someone commits to the process of writing their first book, I give them a very early warning: remember that even well-meaning people, family and friends, can try to steal your dream. Be aware who you listen to. A lot of people who have given up on their dreams can try to discourage you from having yours. Protect your dream and back yourself all the way.

You wouldn't believe how many people walk out excited, ready to take on this journey, and then get shut down by their parent, their spouse, their sister/brother, their friends, or associates. This is one block that is one of the more dangerous ones, especially if you are a person who may not be as self-confident or have low self-worth. You can really buy into the dream stealer's words.

I encourage you to pay attention to this part of the book because there are going to be people who will discourage you as they have given up on something they thought was impossible for themselves.

Sometimes it's actually a great idea not to share what you're doing and then surprise them when it's done. I've certainly had quite a few authors do this – refer to their interviews later, and in the bonus PDF resource. When it's been done, and they've literally walked into their partner with this book, their partner has been overjoyed and so happy and proud of them.

Choose who you tell and when you tell them very carefully. Other people can really look to change our minds, not because it's anything to do with us and that we are incapable, but it's more the fact that they feel that maybe they will be left behind because of this journey.

It is a transformational process; I've said that before and I will say it again. People can feel that you are placing pressure on them to perform, evolve and transform, also. Even for ourselves, if we feel that we will grow on this journey, we may sabotage ourselves because of the feeling that if we grow too much, we won't belong to our original tribe.

One thing that I do see happen is that there might be a little bit of a divergence when someone becomes an author, or they grow beyond their immediate circle in terms of mindset, skills, and abilities, but I believe that the tribe always comes back and encourages and follows you. There is once again a convergence at the other end.

I felt that when I started my business I no longer hung out or talked to people that I normally talked to in terms of family and friends, but once I had reached a level of confidence and success about myself, I was able to come back into the tribe. We were able to relate to each other, and they were proud of me. Just remember, your tribe may not be on your side to begin with, but so long as you step up and prove yourself, your tribe will rejoin you and encourage you to more success.

18. SPOUSAL APPROVAL

Your partner or spouse can be a big road block you need to overcome in terms of having permission from them to take the time and invest the money into writing your first book. One thing that I want you to note here is that if you want the support of your spouse and/or partner, you are the only one who can judge how supportive they are likely to be.

I encourage you to involve them in this journey as much as possible. If you are going to check out a mentor or a program with whom you want to do your book with, take your partner with you to that seminar, take them to that conversation, because it's really hard to reiterate and describe to them what happened in that presentation or conversation.

When I meet people in my events who sit through the four-hour super valuable workshop to fully understand the value behind our Ultimate 48 Hour Author program and process, a large percentage go home and get discouraged or shut down by their partner. It's not easy for someone to understand the value of the investment unless they've sat through that workshop and presentation. All they end up doing is judging the process on the price.

If, in the past, the person who wants to write the first book has invested in things and haven't followed through, and they suffer from what we call 'shiny object syndrome', this can become a real big problem in getting ongoing support from a partner/spouse. In this case, you really need to communicate and be firm in your commitment to this process, because writing your first book can be a very uncertain reality as to whether you'll finish or not. After all, you are doing it for the first time. Will you stick it out with your mindset? Will you deal with the obstacles and the challenges and the fear that will arise, even when you have decided to go through the journey?

Bring along your spouse and the people you are considering helping you write the first book, because when you do that both parties end up being fully supportive of each other, fully understand the process and what's going to happen next, how this may affect their family and finances, and then they make the decision together. It is so much easier, and then the success is guaranteed, especially if you feel that maybe they are not as supportive as other people's partners.

If your partner has always given you independence and an ability to make your own decisions, and you have control over what you do, then of course you can go on your own; you don't need to involve them. If you do need that extra level of support to convince them that this is the right thing for you to do, then take them along. Then you're making an informed decision; you have a second person who has heard the information who may have understood it in a different way, so you can discuss later between one another. They will learn how to further support you through the journey of becoming a first-time author.

19. NO REGRETS!

What will happen if you do nothing about writing your first book? The answer, time and time again, is regret! 70% of my attendees who walk into my half-day workshop say that they have been thinking about writing a book for five years, or more.

As a nice metaphorical intro into the workshop, I play for them a video called *The Miracle of the Chinese Bamboo*. If you haven't seen it or know about it, please watch it on YouTube. I share half of that video at the beginning, and I share the other half at the end of the workshop. It is a perfect and beautiful metaphor for what our business stands for and what it does for people, but also very much a metaphor and an illustration for the things that we really want in life; how they can be under the surface for a long period of time, and then sprout out super-fast when we make the decision to take matters in our own hands.

Regret is one of the biggest things that people feel on their death beds about certain things that they didn't do, and certain chances that they didn't take. This is not where I want people to end up who have that deep desire to write a book. I want you to think about this seriously, because it is something that will eat away at you – these are words I'm using from the answers that people tell me as I speak to them:

- It will eat away at me.
- The music will die still within me.
- I will be frustrated.
- I will be disappointed.
- I won't achieve my bucket list item that I've been dreaming about for so long.

I think this is the strongest feeling when it comes to not writing your book. Things like less opportunities, less income, not as much credibility are mentioned, however, at the top of the list are all of the feelings within you that you will think and feel about yourself if you don't write your book.

Let's not go there; follow through on this dream at least once so that you have something that you can leave for your family, share your philosophy on what you want to write about your life, about your expertise, and the people who you want to help.

20. HEAL FAST

Could the process of writing give you a sense of healing from something that you have overcome? It could be a situation or a lifestyle that you have built because of a certain crisis that has occurred in your life. Perhaps things that you have experienced in your life that you really want to get off your chest?

30% of the people I meet who are on the journey of writing their first book are doing it for this exact reason; to heal their soul and move on with their lives. The reason is that they want to heal through the process. They want to get their experiences out on paper because it has been proven that if you do that you may deal with those emotions and move past them.

Those who write their book on their past feel like they can close off a chapter of the book of their life, and move onto the next one. They find the journey empowering and very therapeutic. Many have come to me needing to firstly heal themselves, even when writing business books, because they have gone through a lot of hard work, persistence, and resilience to get their businesses to a certain level. When they talk about their stories, even about their exploits within their business, they get quite emotional.

When there are more sensitive topics such as domestic violence, divorce, and health problems that they've gone through, high emotions arise that provide amazing healing. Almost every author says that is a huge benefit of going through this process that they didn't even consider when I first designed my program. Others tell me the reason they are writing their book with us is because they want to get through this healing as fast as possible so that they can get on with their life.

Consider that your first book will have an aspect of providing some healing for you around a certain area within your life. It is a benefit that you'll get by going through the process, no matter how boring or dry you may think your topic may be. We have had people who've written on finance and book-keeping which, to many, aren't topics of general interest, yet the development they go through as they pull their expertise together has really given them a huge boost of confidence. It often brings a more human aspect to a topic or a career that someone wouldn't be too interested in reading. Becoming an author and sharing some more personal stories humanises some of the people behind those careers.

Think about it; is your topic going to give you the hidden benefit of healing as you go on this journey to catapult to the next exciting phase of your life?

21. TROLLS ARE REAL

When you write and publish a book, there will be some people who will be highly envious of you. There will be people who will judge you, and those who may criticise you in your industry or on social media. We call them trolls.

How do you deal with trolls? When you go through this process of writing your book a transformation will occur, and as result you grow thicker skin. As you grow thicker skin, these trolls don't tend to bother you much. You have the knowledge that deep down inside you are doing the right thing, you are helping the right people, and the best opportunities are coming to you in your life and your business; your ideal client match.

Whatever you do, don't spark the fire any further. If people do troll and criticise you on social media, don't bite back as it's ultimately not about stooping down to their level, but serving those who have your back. If you want to deal with them, make a personal phone conversation; don't blast it out online in the public forum.

These days other people are very aware of trolls and their behaviour, and have an understanding that it is the troll's insecurities, loneliness, and need to be heard that is driving their poor or aggressive behaviour. Another good thing to remember is unless they have been in the area with you, their opinions don't matter.

My style is to minimise any conflict online, to keep it separate, and to deal with any trolling in the most amicable and friendly way. If you launch personal attacks back and the troll goes out to destroy your reputation online by posting lies and innuendo about you or your business, people who Google you in the future may stumble across this information. It is quite difficult to remove or clean up from online media, even if it is untrue.

If I need to vent, I tend to go to my husband, Stuart, and say all the things that I would want to say to this particular troll. Then I deal with it in a different way after he gives me another perspective. It is good to respond in a positive and resourceful way to the troll, and leave it on social media for others to see how you conduct yourself, often winning you even more fans.

Other people choose to delete comments, because you do have the power of deleting comments off your own profile or post. Also, you can manually approve things that are being posted on your timeline by others, which is a great way to keep track of any trolls.

Look at your privacy and approval settings on your social media profiles and set them to protect your name being taken through the mud in front of your own tribe.

I highly recommend having your settings this way, as occasionally you may have a client who has slipped through your 'No Dickheads' policy. They may feel hard done by, ignored, or worse. Be mindful that you are dealing with those challenging situations where you do disagree with people in the most positive way, even though you might want to tell them to go jump in a river.

Keep it brief, vent to someone you trust, then keep the conversation with those people on social media in the most positive way so that it doesn't blow up your reputation.

It is very important to keep your reputation intact and always act with integrity online. I know for a fact that a few people who have been deciding whether to work with me or not tell me they Googled 'Natasa Denman scam', and 'Ultimate 48 Hour Author scam' because what we do seems almost too good to be true.

22. WHEN ENGLISH IS NOT YOUR MOTHER TONGUE

Growing up in Macedonia and not speaking any English until I was 14, then coming to a country and needing to assimilate into a culture that is English-speaking was one of my early challenges. I had to build the confidence around being able to think on my feet, being able to deliver and now travel worldwide, and speak to audiences from all different cultures. With the background that I have, I tend to attract a lot of other clients for whom English is not their first language, or they even live in a country where English is not the primary language, like the United Arab Emirates. I have worked with more than 15 people from the Middle East now who wrote their books in English, and then translated them to into their native Arabic.

Fluency, not using big enough words, not sounding 'smart enough' … these are the challenges and hesitations that people have when embarking on writing their first book when English isn't their native tongue.

There will be a way of writing your book if you have the desire to do it. We will find a way to get around these challenges, as we have not only worked with people in the Middle East, but also a lot of people here in Australia are multicultural and they have got heavy accents. They're worried about their accents, but at the end of the day, sometimes their written work turns out to be pretty amazing, and as our editors polish it up in the editing process, their work is something they are extremely proud of.

I've often been told by my editors that I switch words around the opposite way they should be because that's the way Macedonian language works. As I've been writing more and more, my editors also say to me my fluency and style has improved significantly, and it's better and better every time I do it.

The old saying that practice makes perfect is so true in this case. Know that you've got experts alongside you to help you refine your words, so don't let this obstacle stand in your way. You will have everything in the correct order, in the correct grammatical position, so this should be relieving to know. Don't put that barrier up just because your spoken English may not be perfect.

Certainly, if you are very rough in English and you don't have a lot of vocabulary, it will be a challenge. The majority of people that I do meet from Asian, Indian, Middle Eastern, and European cultures have an accent, but their English is actually really good, so sometimes they may think that's going to be a challenge with their spoken audio. Our transcriptionist can understand, and can hear accents and transcribe them really well, so that should not be one of the things that's stopping you from taking this journey to the next step of writing your book.

We have helped many people in this situation, and I believe the reason we do so is because of my background; they can see that if I can do it, (this is my 9th book), they can do it for sure.

23. I JUST STARTED MY BUSINESS

There are two ways to look at the choice of writing your book for business purposes. Some people will say, 'Look, you need to really prove yourself and become a bit more famous around what you do, and then you write your book and bring it out.'

My story was the complete opposite. I had one paying client when I decided to write my very first book. I had trialed more than 50-60 marketing strategies to get leads into my business, and nothing was really catching on or being sustainable. By the time my first book came out, I only had two paying clients, and generated $7,000 in revenue after the first 12 months.

I could have given myself the excuse that I don't have enough clients, I haven't done this long enough, or maybe I don't even know enough yet. However, I knew that I had studied human behaviour and mindset, and had gone on my own journey to lose 10 kilos, which was the content for my first book, *The 7 Ultimate Secrets to Weight Loss*.

My belief is, 'Write a book and get famous.' I tend to attract 80% of people who are in this particular category, and a book is really a launch pad for them to be more visible. It helps them build that credibility at a rapid rate, because when people see that you have written a book, they immediately perceive that you've been around for a longer than you actually have been, and must be an expert on your content. That's certainly been my experience from having helped a lot of start-up businesses do their first books.

Certainly, the people who are more established, have their business online, and have a following find the whole process a lot faster and easier. This is, of course, because they have got an established network, and they monetise their book a lot faster with this larger, warm network. My role with the newer business owners is to help them grow that following and credibility rapidly. This is done so that they can then produce results in their first business that's going to give them that ROI in monetising and progressing further a lot faster.

That is also the reasons I have written a book every year around May for the past seven years. It's this time that I get my next book idea and I bring the expertise and views that I have observed over the previous year or years into a neat little package for people to consume.

The excuse of not being established enough in business should not be one that is preventing you from writing your first book. Just know that when the book does come out, you will be able to be recognised and selected over other people who don't have the book, even when they are in the same niche. The perception and reality is that nothing says 'expert' like being a published author.

PART 2

Your Process Questions

24. HIRE HELP FOR YOUR FIRST BOOK

When writing your first book, my biggest tip is to make sure that you do it with someone who has walked that path before, and has helped many people through the same process. This is going to save you a ton of time and money, and make you a lot of money, as well. I wish I had a mentor when I wrote my first book, but I didn't know people like me existed.

Having someone who will be able to show you the shortcuts and the things that actually work, as well as the things that don't work is invaluable. This way you can achieve the maximum leverage and success you can have with your book.

At a keynote speaking gig, or at my half-day event, I share so much of the 'how', but it is actually impossible for me to go into the depth that I do at my retreats, as well as the support that we offer beyond those retreats to our clients.

Often people have this false idea that they will write their book fully by themselves, without any assistance, aside from the publishing process. I know this myself firsthand, because that's how I did my very first book. If I had to do it all over again, I would definitely go with something like what we deliver. Why? Because I made so many mistakes when it comes to lack of marketing my first book and, of course, I took 90 times longer (because now I can do a book in a day, and back then it took me 90 days to write my first book).

I got stung by vanity publishers, something I won't explain in a lot of depth in here, but I do talk about that in my half-day workshop. I lacked savviness around how the book was going to build my business, as I had no one to show and teach me that crucial part of writing a business-style book.

The one thing that did save me was my willingness and ability to go out and network and promote myself, and do all the groundwork. I am great at pounding the pavement. That was the difference that really enabled me to grow my business behind the book because I was physically there, and people were meeting me; that's how I was getting the opportunities.

If you want to leverage the book online and through other strategies that are going to bring new enquiries and business, but are not going to need that face to face connection, then doing it with people who have got those strategies now is very important. Make sure they are doing it for themselves, and are going to give you the answers you need.

When people try to do this themselves, they end up with a book that looks amateur and unprofessional, one that really you can tell is self-published. The goal and the aim is to come up with a traditional, publishing-quality book, but it is a self-published. Make sure the layout looks professional, the design, the quality of the paper, and the way it's all pulled together is what a book should be like; that it looks like it belongs on a shelf in a bookstore. When you walk into bookstores and you look at those books, they're of a high quality. That is what your book needs to mirror for it to have a positive effect on your business and profile.

Please don't do this by yourself for the very first time. Invest in mentorship. You will know in hindsight that you have saved a ton of time and money, as well as received so much more value behind the whole process.

We are passionate not just about helping people finish their first book, but about all of the content and information about what to do with their book beyond its publishing. That is where we see the biggest value in our first-time authors through the program.

The ones who already have established businesses see the value in having it executed so rapidly, and in having all the experts that we know, like, and trust, and have tested hundreds of times over. The ones that do want to seriously build that business behind it see that attending the retreat and the further marketing masterclasses that we deliver to our clients as invaluable.

Get someone to show you the ropes; after that, you can do it yourself over and over again. That is also our ultimate intention; that our authors do not need to buy our program each time (apart from the publishing package). They actually are investing in a system that is replicable, and they repeat the process themselves so they can be many times published authors in the future.

25. SAVING MONEY COSTS MONEY IN THE LONG RUN

I don't know if you have purchased a sub-quality product in the past, but my husband and I used to buy cheap vacuum cleaners. Every year, or maybe within 18 months of buying that cheap vacuum cleaner, we would find ourselves back in a store buying a replacement. This went on for a number of years; I think we went through five vacuum cleaners in about seven or eight years, and as we were buying a new home we decided that enough was enough – let's spend on quality. Quality that's going to last us 10-20 years, and we don't need to think about replacing it. It's actually going to give us a better outcome in terms of what our home feels like and the appliances that we use in it long-term.

We invested in Miele appliances for our dishwasher, washing machine, dryer, and vacuum cleaner. We've been in our current home now for three and a half years, and none of those appliances even feel like they are a day old. Trying to skimp and save money on the process of writing a book and doing these things by yourself is guaranteed to deliver a sub-quality product that's missing a lot of components.

If you don't invest in someone who knows this whole process from start to finish, you might end up with a book that isn't a reflection of who you are, or the vision you had for it. Not only that, it's also going to cost you a lot of time. Time is money nowadays. Recently I was at a convention, and a lady who wrote her book about 15 years ago stood up and talked about her year of hell pulling together her book because she was trying to do all the components herself; the illustrations, buying the ISBN numbers, the editors, the layout, and things that she just had no idea were going to arise on pulling together this project.

Even though the investment may be higher to go with someone who's going to give you something from start to finish, there is no point writing a book if you don't know how to publish it, just as there is no point buying a publishing package if you don't know how to write it or market it.

I believe the investment is well worth it because the return on investment at the other end is going to pay for the up-front costs. This is due to the fact you'll be doing things the right way, and you are going to be saving time because you're not trying to make all the pieces of the puzzle fit all by yourself.

Look at quality, look at people who have great reputation, and people who have helped a lot of others become first-time authors, and then get your hand held all the way. You are an expert in your field; I am sure you don't try to fix your plumbing by yourself, so remember once you've done it the first time, you will be able to start taking the same steps within your own hands.

If you value your time, for the first book you write and publish it is really important to invest in a system that's going to show you the ropes so that you can replicate it in the future for your other books – believe me, writing them becomes addictive.

26. UNFORGETTABLE EXPERIENCE

Writing your first book is a very special time, just like having your first child. It's something that you will remember forever. I always remember who I did it with, why I decided to do it, and I'm forever grateful – even though, in hindsight, I didn't choose to engage with the right company for my very first book.

What is it that you want to remember about writing your first book? Is it purely the writing process and how you went through all of this? Or do you want to have a memorable experience? My whole intention with creating the Ultimate 48 Hour Author retreats was to provide a lifelong memory. It was going to not just be about writing the book and learning how to leverage it, but to also develop those lifelong friendships and connections. Can you remember any trips or experiences where you have met some people, maybe on a cruise or a Contiki tour, and you've forever stayed friends, connected through that process that you reminisce about years later?

By taking up to 20 people away on these retreats, they connect and develop close-knit bonds and collaborations in their businesses, as well as achieving their goal of writing their first book. One of the upsides of being away together at a retreat is we can do certain exercises and activities that really make the nights memorable in the social side of the retreat.

We are always making it relevant to what we're doing, such as the pre-launch of the books on the Friday night, and the excitement and squeals as they sell their first few books (162 books is the most that's been sold at our prelaunch over the 48-hour period of retreat). The experience of 'birthing' your first book is something that you will remember, and it's a choice how you do it, whether you do it alone or with a group of people, or you go on a writing retreat.

Decide what it is that you want to do, make it special, mark that time in your planner, take yourself away, and execute the content of your book away from your daily distractions.

What's special about this book is I actually started it on my birthday, so it is something I will always remember. I was at the cinemas on my own, and in the last 10 minutes of the movie I got an idea. I had to drive home rapidly just to get it all down on paper and start speaking it out. I was so excited to get this book in the hands of those who need it as soon as possible. I will always remember that I wrote this book on my 41st birthday, and the crazy 24 hours that I executing its content.

It's really rewarding, and it will remain a memorable experience. That's how I would like to think about it in the years to come.

To check out what our author experience actually looks like, check out this video: http://bit.ly/Ultimate48HourAuthor

27. BESTSELLER BULLSHIT

Being a bestseller is every author's dream. It makes us look more credible, and it makes us seem on that next level of authorship. In today's world, I call bullshit on it. Being a bestseller has been bastardised with hacks in place to manipulate the system and become a bestselling author by default.

To become a bestselling author in Australia for a paperback book, it's said that you need to sell 5,000 copies of your book. Guess what – the way people are becoming bestsellers is that they are purchasing their own books as they are going to print. So, you could get your cousin to get invoiced for 5,000 books, you give them the money, and then that book has been printed in 5,000 copies and 'purchased'. It becomes a bestselling book, and you a bestselling author.

Companies who value this bestseller status get people to do exactly this, and for some people it is what they want, as deceptive as it is. People who pull together contributor books get 10 people to be part of it who all invest [X] amount of money, get 500 copies printed, and boom – that book becomes a bestseller.

This is actually my story, before I even knew that things like this went on in the writing and publishing world. I was invited to be a contributor into one book; the investment was $3000, and for that I would get 500 copies of the book with my chapter inside. I didn't realise that this was a strategy, so when the books came they told me what we'd done. It almost made me sick!

The second type of bestseller that a lot of people are aware of (and we can see it in a lot of people's speaker bios and profiles) is the Amazon #1 bestselling author. Again, it's just a hack – a process and strategy. You simply hire people to execute this strategy for you to launch a book on Amazon, and set up a campaign to sell as many copies of your book as possible in just 24 hours.

The simple way to explain this process is that your book gets put on Amazon in a subcategory that doesn't have a lot of competition. You pick a launch date, and as you lead up to that date you are told to tell all your nearest and dearest, and your network, to support you in the launch of your book. When the date arrives, your book gets dropped to $0.99 and so long as you have sold the most books in that 24-hour period, you get your beautiful golden Amazon bestselling stamp for life. You can claim that as one of your credibility building things when people introduce you, even if you don't sell another book on Amazon ever again when you put your book back to the RRP.

In my eyes, the true bestsellers are books that end up on the *New York Times* bestseller list, like the *Harry Potter* books, *Rich Dad, Poor Dad*, etc. ... those books that we have all heard of before and we know many people have read them. As much as I do believe, yes, a credibility stamp that says you're a bestselling author is going to be awesome even if it is deceptive, people who haven't read this would think that you are more credible as a bestseller.

The process behind how this is done is quite dodgy, and lacking integrity. That's why I'm not personally a big fan of it, even after being through it myself by accident, but each to their own. Certainly if you want to build your credibility further, and you want to use this strategy, then go for it – but that is what really truly happens when we're speaking of bestsellers.

28. WHY EBOOKS ALONE SUCK

The question often arises about the value of an eBook as opposed to a paperback. The reality is, we are starting to live in a more electronic world and people are not buying paperback books as much as they did even five years ago. People are consuming books through Kindle and audiobooks. So many wannabe first-time authors often ask the question, 'Couldn't I just write an eBook? Why do I need to go through the expensive process of pulling together a book that's going to be printed, then have to physically store it, and move this sometimes heavy product around?'

We live in a physical world, and the perception of value and credibility that a physical book gives you is something you'll never have from an eBook. A book makes a noise when you drop it. An eBook makes no sound; it has no 'thud value'. People don't perceive eBooks to be of high value at all. Many feel as if you've just put some content into a PDF that you send through to someone else to consume.

I believe, even if you don't sell a lot of physical books, that you should still have your book available in its physical form because when you are going out and meeting people, speaking events, or running workshops, you want to give them something physical, especially if you are in a service-based industry.

Physical gifts give the 'wow' factor. They can be set up on tables as your branding and display piece at your events, and included as a value-add to a program or package. You will sell more of them as when people meet you they will want to take something away. In my experience when people have met me and received a signed book from me, they are less likely to throw it out. I know I keep all books where I have actually met the author.

You certainly should convert your book into an eBook. An eBook requires a whole conversion process on its own, and needs its own ISBN number, in addition to the ISBN number for your physical book. It can then be converted into an audiobook, yet another way to generate revenue from your content. That's become very popular amongst readers who prefer to listen to an audiobook in the car, while travelling, or simply doing things around the house.

I recommend you have on-hand at least 100 copies of your books and then print them on-demand, so you don't necessarily need to keep reprinting or have a ton of books in your garage. Do keep one box in the boot or your car and one book in your bag at all times so that whenever you're meeting and introducing yourself to people, you can give them that as a business card on steroids.

29. TYPING VS. SPEAKING

Have you ever considered that you can speak out your book in just five hours? Five hours of recorded audio translates to around 40,000 words on the written page. This is a significantly shorter period of time than typing it out, and gives fluidity and a conversational style to the final product. This is how we do it at Ultimate 48 Hour Author.

Of course, speaking out a book will contain some idiosyncrasies that we all have in our speech. This is why you'll need to clean up that transcript once it comes back to you from the transcriptionist. Certainly not every single person is a natural-born speaker, so it can be a little bit daunting when you find yourself in front of a recorder needing to perform. For our clients who are practitioners, coaches, or professional speakers, the system works wonderfully well. For those who don't do much speaking, we coach them through the process.

I always teach my clients to get in the zone; allow your content and stories to just flow through you with the aid of your pages of cheat notes in front of you. That way you're guided by the structure and process of what you're speaking about. Trust that after practicing a few times you will become a little bit more familiar and comfortable with recording yourself. Ultimately, it's about you simply delivering your story, your presentation, and your content in front of a client or an audience – they're just not speaking back to you.

Typing can have therapeutic affects for people, so typing is the alternative way that some of my authors choose to do this. It will take a lot longer to complete this the traditional way, which is what most people worry about. Not everyone is blessed to have the skills of touch-typing and doing it super-fast. This is one of the reasons a lot of people don't ever finish their book.

If you choose to type, it can feel a lot more connected with the way the book is looking, and you can see that visual outcome of your words on paper, as opposed to an audio file. I recommend if you are going to choose one or the other, stick with your chosen tone and delivery. The way people are reading it will be quite different if you chop and change between typing and speaking your book.

Some benefits with spoken books are that they can be read twice as fast, they do come across very conversational, and are easy to read and understand because we don't use as much complicated language as we would when we type. People don't get stuck on certain areas that they may do in a typed-out book.

Another benefit is that it's a lot more authentic and real. It removes the temptation of copying someone else or accidentally cutting and pasting content, especially in the personal development and 'self-help' books. It reduces the risk of plagiarism because it's your words, said in your flavour and understanding.

When people meet you, they'll feel like they are still listening to you when they read your book. When people meet me at my half-day event or speaking gigs and then read Ultimate 48 Hour Author, or any of my other books, they say it was exactly as if I were speaking at them, like they were at another seminar.

'All the best, whichever way you do it,' I always say to my authors. 'I don't care, as long as you cross that finish line with that first book in hand.'

30. WINNING TOPIC SELECTION

As human beings, we have learnt, studied, and lived through many vast experiences. Perhaps you're one of those people who have many different interests, experiences, and expertise, and you have a lot of ideas when it comes to writing a book. I'm in the same boat, however, the topic selection for your first book should be one that you think about very carefully. When you're starting out you want to make the biggest impact and be able to get a return on investment.

If you're overwhelmed with so many ideas and angles, speak to someone who can look ahead and plan out a bigger vision with what's going to happen beyond the book. How can your book be monetised, how will it be marketed, and what else will you offer beyond your book that can be of value to people? I always say, 'Write the topic and the book that is going to help you monetise your profile and business first before you doing any passion project books such as poetry, children's books, community books, or even fiction or fantasy writing.'

Books such as these are the ones that you will enjoy writing, but if you want to write a book to monetise think self-help, how-to, or expertise-style books. These passion project books will not help you get as much revenue into your business. If you want to transition out of a career into your own business through the book and the credibility that it gives you, do the topic that is most aligned with the expertise that you have.

Think about the how-to book you may be able to write, or a personal life story – what are the lessons in them that you can expand into online programs, or other ways to deliver to an audience? That is the topic selection that I would encourage a first-time author to go with.

I know that it can be quite overwhelming, but don't worry, there is going to be time to write all the books that you want to write. This book was never on my radar when I started writing my first book, but I always made everything that I do very strategically-aligned with what would be fun for me, as well as what's going to be good for the business and to help even more people. The whole reason behind writing this book is to add the extra component that I have felt is a serious gap in the market. This is the book that closes that gap between just thinking about writing the first book and actually going through with it.

31. CONTENT SHY

I was one of those people who didn't believe they had enough information in their head to be able to write a book. I meet those individuals all the time on my tours who say, 'Nat, I just don't know if I've got enough information that would fill out a book.'

When we get to chatting I tell them that I was in the same exact situation. When finishing my first book I felt that I had emptied my whole brain into that one book, and that there was nothing else left to share. Once you understand how to develop content and how to structure it correctly, you will be gifted with a tool that enables you to be able to develop content over and over again. It will make you believe that the content you have is unlimited. The only limitation that is there is the one that we put on ourselves.

I remember when my husband took over the content writing part within our weight-loss business, developing emails, and writing valuable posts and blog pieces. In the first 12 months that he was doing that, he said to me, 'What happens when I eventually write about everything there is to write about when it comes to weight loss?'

By this stage I had been writing content myself for two and a half years, and I explained to him, 'You can never run out of content. If you need inspiration, go on YouTube, go read a few blog pieces on the particular topic, and see if you have an a-ha moment. Then see if you can spin that moment within your own blog piece, or an email that you want to write to the audience.'

There's always inspiration that we can get from videos and podcasts and other people's blogs. I certainly don't encourage anyone to copy other people's ideas or models, but you can get inspiration if you're feeling like you're running dry on ideas. The other way is to just look at your own life. If you are the expert at what you're writing about and you're sharing that knowledge with people, the things that you're doing on a daily basis should give birth to ideas for blogging or live streaming. You are creating further content pieces for what you really love, as the topic of your first book is the one that you're fully-obsessed about, something you think about all the time. This is generally why you want to write that first book.

Content is unlimited; you do have enough, and if you don't you can get inspiration and write things in your own words with your own insights. Look at your own life in terms of what is happening around you, and how you can convert that into a story or a content piece.

32. CONTENT OVERLOAD

Many of my event attendees say, 'I've been writing for many years and I just have so much information I don't know what to do with.' They sometimes even bring in bags of printed content, chapters that they've written, or they show me on their computer. This is probably the tougher situation to be in, rather than the one where you feel like you may not have enough content to write a book. People can feel like they've had so much life experience and they've got so many ideas that they want to share, but how do they pick what to leave out and what to put in?

If you're overwhelmed and you proceed to write in that space, feeling that way, you're going to make your reader overwhelmed. The best thing I encourage people to do who come to me with a lot of pre-written stuff is to scrap it all and begin with a brand new book unpack. I show them how to then unpack, and develop the content around this new book. This will still entail some of those aspects they've been writing about all over the place, but what it does is that it will bring structure and order to it.

My recommendation is that you keep things as simple as possible. It's impossible to share with someone absolutely everything you know in one single book; you just don't have enough time or space. The reality is you don't want to overwhelm your reader, because a confused mind will always say no. My recommendation has always been to pick the top three key points you may want to share with your reader around a particular how-to topic, or whatever it is that you're sharing within each of your chapters, because the brain loves threes. This way it doesn't feel overwhelmed. Then you can leave the remainder of the information to be delivered in further content like your online courses, when you're working with people more in-depth, intensive trainings, group masterminds, and coaching.

'Keep it simple, stupid,' (KISS) is an important part of writing your very first book because if people feel that what they're reading just seems all too hard they're never going to take the next steps with you. You want to make things appear achievable, as the brain is always looking for the path of least resistance; the ability to achieve a goal in the shortest time possible with the least amount of pain.

For those of you who have too much information, too much content, distil it; start from scratch, and get it out there. You may be able to use some of that information that you've written down, but really, that could have been just your initial drafts. Now you're ready to pull it together in a nice, organised fashion.

Choose the topic that is going to best benefit your brand and business, if that's what you're doing it for. If it an autobiographical book, develop it in chronological order and then pull it together in the simplest way that you possibly can. If it's too all over the place, just start from the beginning and speak it out. As I said, it's a lot easier for people to consume when the content is more conversational.

33. STARTING POINT

'What are your biggest challenges when you think about writing a book?' When I ask this, in the top three is always the starting point – first-time authors just don't know where to start. This is a valid one, because if you've never written a book before it can be daunting. Where do you start? There is so much you most likely want to share, and you end up having no idea what to do.

This is a more of a strategy or a process challenge to address, rather than a mindset one. First of all, make sure you address the mindset behind starting your book – have you worked on the fear of not being good enough, increasing your self-worth? If you have addressed these mindset obstacles and gotten over yourself, you'll find the resources – look up information on Google, and buy books like *Ultimate 48 Hour Author.*

The easiest strategy and process that I can share with you is to start with the book unpack. I like to teach people to write 12 chapters because that can be leveraged to further products; a 12-module online course, a 12-week program, a 12-month program. It can be converted into 12 webinars, or keynotes, and the information can be duplicated and delivered in so many formats.

As you can see, this particular book has 48 mini-chapters because it was written to address most of the challenges and obstacles that people encounter when it comes to writing their first book. The intention is so people can pick and choose the ones that apply to them the most. There really isn't a rule how many chapters you need to have, but if you're going to build a system with your book then think about the 12-chapter strategy.

If you want to observe this particular process of how it's done, just email us via the contact information at the back of the book. We can have you attend one of our half-day events where we do it live in the room. If you're not in the city where we can meet face-to-face, as we can talk about sharing some professional footage where you can observe that for a smaller investment, instead of attending the live event.

I am more than happy to share with you the book unpack template, however, it's really important that you actually watch how the process unfolds. You can see a template and think that, 'Oh yeah, this is easy, I can do this,' but unless you know the workings behind why that template has been put together the way we have done it, it's really difficult to follow completely on your own.

Start from the big picture (the book skeleton), then break things down further into smaller chunks. If you are still not biting the bullet and getting started, then address if the starting point challenge is really your roadblock, or if it's your mindset. Mindset comes first, process comes second.

34. STRUCTURE MATTERS

After the starting point, the next challenge is structure and flow. People say, 'I just think I'm going to repeat myself or be all over the place. How do I make sure that the book comes up in an orderly fashion that's easy to understand so that people enjoy reading it?'

What comes next is what I've called the Ultimate Chapter Unpack system. This is where you break down your chapter into the information that you'll be talking about in an orderly fashion. You'll have your stories, facts, or reasons about the particular topic. This can vary from book to book, because not every book is in the how-to genre. We have a how-to chapter unpack template, and we have a personal story chapter unpack template. This is more chronological. I sometimes even invent a chapter unpack template for an author if I feel we need to approach their content differently. It's a creative process, and that is why simply getting access to these templates will not make much sense to you.

My strategy is to answer those questions that people ask me time and time again, and address the comments that I receive from people who are yet to become first-time authors. I know my information really intimately; I answer these questions multiple times, I have a little spiel about it. I'm sure if you're an expert at your topic or you really know what you're talking about, just a few notes on a page (what I like to call your cheat notes) will pull together in order to deliver content.

If you are executing something with more detail and depth then using the chapter unpack template is a great way to put more of those cheat notes down in a logical sequence. It gives you that structure to pull together chapter after chapter, avoiding repetition.

At the end of the day, once you have executed your content, the recommendation is to check out any other books out there in your niche. Look at the layout of that book and put it in that particular order. Can you notice a pattern or sequence? The order of a book layout might be: testimonials first up, a dedication, then your introduction, chapters, afterword, about the author, and finally you may have offers at the back of the book with some more testimonials.

Realistically it's about deciding on a flow that will work for you, as people will have different ways that they unpack content. That's why I have few chapter unpack templates. Once again, structure is a process challenge. The processes I've described have been written about in detail in *Ultimate 48 Hour Author*. That it is not the true problem here; it is more about what is it that you need to get through within yourself to give yourself the permission to write your very first book.

35. BORROW CREDIBILITY

It's really important to collect testimonials for your book content from clients that you've worked with in your business. When you collect testimonials, you need to get permission for it to be published in your book. Via email is suitable.

The trick to testimonials is to keep them nice and short. Someone may give you half a page of feedback on you as a business owner, or on your book content, but I encourage you to pull out the two or three sentences that are the most powerful, then send it back to them for approval. I advise you to put these testimonials at the beginning of the book, and you might like to put a page of them towards the back just before your offers, as another form of credibility.

If you know people in your industry who are quite influential and have high credibility ask for them for a testimonial, or to write a foreword for your book. Make sure that person is known and famous in your niche and industry. If you were writing a weight-loss book and Michelle Bridges was able to be give you a foreword, that would be something that you can leverage further – add a stamp on the cover of the book saying, 'Foreword written by Michelle Bridges.' This is how you borrow someone else's credibility through your own book, thus boosting the interest others will have in it.

In the marketplace we have seen people co-author books with famous influential people, like Brian Tracy. My partner in Dubai, Moustafa Hamwi, co-authored a book with Dr Marshall Goldsmith. This is another way of positioning and borrowing someone else's credibility that they've worked very hard and long for to leverage your own.

Remember to ask your clients to write you testimonials regularly. Video is always best as you can transcribe it. Do ask before they go into a book that you can use them in that way. Most people would be delighted to have their name in a book.

When is the right the time to get a testimonial for your book? I suggest going through the first round of editing, and then send that draft copy to people who you want to testify for you. Sometimes people read the whole book, sometimes they'll read parts of it, but so long as they're satisfied with the content that they're endorsing they will give you something in return. Ensure that you address confidentiality around your book content and that you give it to those you trust.

Aim for 10 testimonials. You can have a combination of character references or client testimonials, as well as book content-related testimonials.

36. YOU ARE A CREATIVE GENIUS – THAT IS NOT THE PROBLEM!

'I'm not all that creative,' is one of the things that I hear often. I just want to call you on your BS if this is your excuse. We are all born very creative, and sometimes it is our creativity that gets us more into trouble. We want to try this, we want to try that, we have this idea, and we keep changing and swapping because our creativity is at an all-time high. People who have 'shiny object syndrome' end up switching from one project to another, a highly un-resourceful way of living life and building a successful business. In my first 12 months of my business, it wasn't the lack of creativity or ideas or actions that was holding me back; it was the lack of focus that was preventing me from getting further ahead in creating a sustainable or viable business.

We are all creative creatures. There's no lack of creativity in this world, there is a lack of focus. I want you to really think about that. If you keep jumping from one idea to the next, it means that your creativity is being sparked and getting you excited. It's like a drug. It's exciting when a brand new idea arises, but following that idea to completion is where a lot of people fail.

The famous saying, 'Get in line and stay in line' is so true for those people who do reach success and finish their very first books. If you keep chopping and changing, or moving around deck chairs and deciding on a different angle or different topic, you will never reach the finish line. It's not the lack of creativity that gets people into trouble, it's the inability to Follow One Course Until Successful (FOCUS).

Stop saying that you're not creative. You are creative; just work on developing your 'focus muscle'. Decide on your topic, and your timeline, and then execute until you are holding your first book in hand. You can then replicate the same process time and time again for future books. Get in line and stay in line! Doing too many things all at once is not going to mean that you're going to be that much more successful, or make more money. There is a great book called *The One Thing* – look it up, it describes this way of thinking and being beautifully.

Go forth, stay focused, and believe that you have everything within you that you need when it comes to creativity.

37. JUST START WRITING

People ask me, 'What have you studied? How have you developed your writing skills? Have you done a literary degree? Was your degree at university in journalism?' I say, 'No, it wasn't. I have never done any formal writing or learning around the know-how of structure content.'

I did not speak English until I was 14, because I was raised in Macedonia. I spoke Macedonian, which is a Slavic language. When I came here I did not want to open my mouth because I was too scared I would make a mistake speaking English. As I learnt English and grew through this journey of developing my speaking skills, I continued to speak and speak (I ended up being a bit of a chatterbox).

That is why say to people, 'If you can speak, you can write.' It is ideal if can make your writing style as close as possible to the way you speak, as if you're having a conversation. What that means is that more people will understand you and be more open to absorbing the information you are sharing. Just like you're reading this book now, you can read it a lot faster. People get through the information a lot easier, and you use words that are not as complicated, which means more people are likely to really get what you are trying to get across.

I tend to say certain words more often when I speak that are not required in my written work. Once I do the cleanup of my transcripts, the book goes through an editing process and gets further tidied up, and put into an awesome readable format.

You don't have to have a literary degree; a little bit of practice with speaking is all you need. Speaking out your book does not need to be perfect. Please don't judge yourself on your tone of voice if you're listening to your recording. I strongly recommend that you leave that to the side, because sometimes you're thinking about what you're going to say next. You're not going to sound like you're speaking on a stage, where you will have a lot more personality and zest in delivering your message. It's more about how it appears on the paper, and then you adjust it further during the cleanup.

You can get this done in as little as five hours of speaking, equaling a 40,000-word book. This is a standard, average-sized book. If you choose to type a book over speaking it, then continue typing it. Don't switch from one to the other.

38. POWER OF THE MASTERMIND

Writing your very first book is a team effort. There are a lot of people who end up being involved in pulling this whole project together for you. That is why you may have noticed many thank you notes and acknowledgements in the back of books. They say it takes a village to raise a child, and I would further that to say that it takes a village to pull together a book.

That is why Ultimate 48 Hour Author, a retreat-style program, came to life. I knew that even though people have this romanticised idea that they should be sitting in a log cabin writing their book for months on end, in reality the easiest way to write your very first book is when you are doing it with people who are on this same journey as you; people who are going through the same challenges, obstacles, and can encourage you and support you along the way.

Completing your book in a group dynamic really gives birth to the power of the mastermind. As we were created to have a tribal mentality, this support really propels us forward. I believe it fast-tracks the process 10-times more than if you were just doing it by yourself remotely.

One of my pet hates in my business is when wannabe first-time authors ask to execute my program remotely, which we do offer in really unique cases – like someone who is unable to travel due to a disability, or they are simply way too far away from Melbourne. The second one is, once again, a matter of how important this is to you – I've had people fly in from the US and UAE to do their retreats (that's a 15 hour flight across the world for them).

My highest preference is for people to be there at the retreat. It is just 48 hours, it doesn't impact people's lives significantly, and the experience and the camaraderie that gets developed is quite intense. Those 48 hours feel like a week because we are doing something significant. It's second to none. I highly recommend that you go away with people and do this together, if you are not going to do a program such as ours. Do it with others and then stay in touch with each other, and push one another to completion. It gives you that accountability.

What we do with our retreat groups is we set up a message in Facebook Messenger 30 days out from the retreat. They get to know each other in the lead up by sharing how their prep is going. This message stays open beyond the retreat until people finish their books, and beyond. The groups create friends for life and a community that they can keep tapping into for different tips and strategies for further leveraging and marketing their book.

The masterminding that occurs, and the questions that get asked helps them feel that they're not alone, that other people are going through exactly the same stuff as they are. This is key when writing your first book. I wouldn't have it any other way. Once you've done it, of course you can do all the stuff on your own, but for your first book, do find a way to do it within a community or a group.

39. TRICK YOURSELF

I said that the cure to procrastination was to make a commitment to someone else. The reason our program has had such a huge success rate in the number of people who follow through and write their first books is because we like to trick them, in two ways.

One way is that we get them to presell their book on the Friday night of the retreat. How this happens is that they arrive at retreat with their content unpacked, but they have not yet verbally delivered that content. The book is still 3-4 months away from being finished. The presale is to trick them out of procrastinating and get them moving towards that finish line. We create a mock-up cover for their books, a 3D image of a book that is physically not yet finished. This may not be the final version of their cover, and their title and tagline may change further along the process.

We get them to create a landing page, or at the very least a PayPal link button that they can share with their community and network to start preselling their book. People can see a visual of the book, what the book is about, and ask for support from their network via their social media platforms or email list.

The whole thinking behind this is to start generating early revenue from the book to start paying back the process of creating the book. Even more so, it is about the author really making it real for themselves and committing, not just to us as their mentors and the group that they're doing it with, but also to their nearest and dearest, who are now championing them to success.

The prelaunch is a really important part, and if you do want to trick yourself in this way, it's very simple to do. Just hire someone on www.fiverr.com to create a 3D image of what your mock-up cover will look like. Supply them with an image of what you want to have on your cover, and then create a PayPal button. I'm sure you can look up on YouTube how this is done. That way you will be able to set something up to prelaunch your book.

I did a Facebook live stream whilst writing this book to say that I was super excited about my next book. I didn't even reveal what it was about, just a little teaser, and there were so many people asking where the prelaunch button was, and the link to pre-purchase. I always pre-launch my books and have a certain following who always buy what I create simply because they love all my content.

I do want to fund this process through the pre-sales of the book, rather than my personal money. I love showing my first-time authors how to pre-launch a book, so that I can also not worry as much about the costs and get encouraged that there are people out there who will support them. Presale is the best way to trick yourself.

The other trick that we have in the Ultimate 48 Hour Author program is that your commitment to this program is end to end. We have pulled together all the experts involved in this process, and deliver the whole experience as a high-value, all-inclusive package that gets you to the point of book-in-hand, as well as mentorship and a high-level community to be a part of for life.

Our program is a high-end retreat. 9/10 people finish it successfully. That is a massive completion rate when you look at other programs that get only 3% follow through rate, as they are only providing parts of authoring a book. We keep it simple, in the one place, with people who have been vetted and tested almost 300 times now.

40. TO TRUST, OR NOT TO TRUST

Writing a book for the very first time is a little bit like putting a jigsaw puzzle together. You have to figure out where all the pieces fit, and what the rules are around creating it. When I meet first-time authors, they aren't aware of what the whole process is, more so when it comes to the publishing industry. One of their common fears is they just don't know who to trust. Some people in the publishing space promise this, and other people promise that, so who do I listen to, and what is the right way to go about this?

Unless you are working with someone who has done this before, and they can give you the insider secrets behind the intentions, every publisher and every company that does help you write a book has got a different intention. Some of them may have the intention of keeping your book just being produced by them, therefore needing to reprint from them at extraordinary costs. This is where they get a lot of their revenue in all of your future dealings. Reprint reruns, as well as wanting to sell you marketing packages, can be super expensive. This is their business model.

Traditional publishers' main intention is to sell a ton of books, and they only take on projects that their gut tells them will sell well.

They do an initial launch, and then you're left to your own devices to do the rest of the marketing for yourself. In some cases with traditional publishers you can get stuck after they have got you to sign off your book rights to them. It could end up being six figures to buy your own rights back.

With Ultimate 48 Hour Author, our intention is to help you leverage your book to build your profile and credibility, rather than focus on a $30 book sale. It's not so much that we don't focus on book sales because we believe that there's not a lot of money in books, but the money is in the leverage, the credibility, the positioning, and business-building strategies you can implement behind your book.

You have to be very mindful about your rights and what you give up, and who you decide to work with. At the end of the day, it could either mean being stuck with a publishing partner who you don't enjoy or is harassing you to spend more money on marketing and promotional opportunities.

I found myself in that situation, getting harassed with marketing and sales phone calls for almost seven years after my first book was released. I continuously said, 'NO', as my focus was on building my business on the back of the book. I was not interested in anything further, which made me republish my book elsewhere, incurring some extra expenses, having it done locally and with full control over my book and my content.

Talk to people who have been through the publishing process, if you are going to do it yourself. Reach out to people who have been published by different companies, and ask about their experience, what it was like, and how much support they had so you can decide what path to go down.

That's the best way to get some honest feedback on the journey, rather than just jumping in with someone you've only spoken to over the phone. These days there are a lot of very experienced salespeople who prey on the vulnerable, who may make everything seem rosy and amazing, and make you feel like you will be the next JK Rowling.

41. LEGAL WORRIES BUSTED

One of the things that people do get a bit worried about when it comes to writing their book, especially if it's a personal story, is around the legality of speaking about other people – especially when those people aren't portrayed in a positive light. I'm only going to talk a little bit about this here as I am not a legal expert.

I want to cover off the main questions that arise, but for further legal advice, seek the expert knowledge of a lawyer. Also, your editor should be able to flag things that potentially might be putting you in danger in the legal aspect of it, and recommend how you can reword or frame things differently.

The main thing to understand if you are speaking about someone else, even if you are changing their name, if they can recognise themselves in the way that you've portrayed them in the book, they can still sue you for slander. Changing their name doesn't mean you're fully protecting yourself.

Other legal things that you need to be aware of are the copyright of images and models that other people may have spoken about in books. Do not copy names of models that other people have used or developed and talk about them as if you have invented them yourself, such as Maslow's Hierarchy of Needs, or similar.

Often we get so many ideas from other books or content watching YouTube, or reading blogs, but you are not to cut and paste information or to discuss certain models, because most likely these models have been trademarked and then you'll be in breach of copyright.

A way around this if you like to use a certain expert's model is to think about how you can rename it so that it is yours, and then put your own personal spin on that information. I'm sure we all love different models, but we change them up because we think something's missing; we can add something, remove something, and make it unique and our own.

After all, in the world today, there's nothing new. People are regurgitating similar information, just delivered with a more modern approach. For example, Tony Robbins used to learn from Brian Tracy and Jim Rohn. He developed models similar to theirs', but renamed them in the Tony Robbins flavour. Other people who love Tony Robbins might teach stuff that Tony Robbins delivers, but in their own flavour as they have their own understanding they can teach best.

You do not need to get permission for using quotes, you just need to credit the person who said it. You do need to get permission if you are sharing more than a couple of sentences from somebody. The hardest approval to get is sharing song lyrics or poems, as they are covered by the strongest copyright laws imaginable. Please avoid using these in your book if they are not your own.

As I mentioned earlier in this chapter, your editor should be able to flag some things that might be in breach legally. My advice is when you are talking about other people, make it more about you and what you've learned on the journey, rather than making someone be portrayed in a really bad light.

42. PUBLISHING DEMYSTIFIED

The publishing industry is definitely one industry that is of a greater concern to people who have never published a book before. I could write a whole book around this industry, but here I want to just give you some distinctions around traditional publishing vs. self-publishing.

Traditional publishing is when a house, like Penguin, Wiley, or Hay House, picks up your book because they think it's an awesome manuscript and they can foresee that this book is going to have great sales. They need to sell a lot of books. They fund the process at the front end for the author, and in some cases, they pay an advance if the author is a celebrity or person of influence with an already large following. One thing to understand, however, is that they don't help you write your book.

A lot of first-time authors will not get picked up by traditional publishers. It is very unlikely unless, as mentioned above, you are a celebrity. There's a lot of rejection in this process, as they do have a lot of control over how the book looks and sounds. Realistically it can take 2-3 years if your book gets accepted to actually put it through the whole traditional publishing process.

If you are impatient, like me, and you want to write your book as quickly as possible, traditional publishing is your worst option. If you want to get your book done fast so you can use it to leverage your brand, to get something looking exactly the way you want it because this is your dream project, something that's on your bucket list, then self-publishing is definitely the alternative route to do it.

Of course, self-publishing means that you will be managing or organising the entire process yourself, and you will need to fund that process. There's varying amounts of investment that need to be considered when self-publishing, however, you are in control of the process and you are guaranteed to become an author because you're funding this process yourself.

With Ultimate 48 Hour Author, we have an aspect of self-publishing as we don't rely on a traditional publishing houses picking up our authors' books. Our package is not purely based on the publishing process, as we actually mentor the writer to get a book that they are proud of. We help with structure, we give you steps, we teach you marketing, we teach you leveraging, and you do it in a community and as part of a retreat program, rather than completely on your own.

Publishing is definitely a bit of a mysterious area when it comes to writing that first book. Once you have chosen your type of publishing, it is really easy to replicate the process, like anything in life. I suggest for the very first book that you get as much help as possible, because that will make your future books higher quality, and a lot easier to finish.

PART 3

Your Process Questions

43. IT'S NOT ABOUT WRITING YOUR FIRST BOOK

There's a quote that I came up with about four years ago, because the more and more I observed people becoming first-time authors, I realised that it actually wasn't so much about the book:

'It's not about writing your first book – it's about the person you become at the other end of it.'
— Natasa Denman

This whole process of backing yourself: increasing your self-worth, overcoming your self-doubt, finding the time, devoting the time and resources, being consistent and disciplined, going through your information, pulling it all together, and project managing bits and pieces can be challenging, but when I held my first book in hand, it gave me a huge boost of confidence. It made me grow a few inches taller, and I presented myself, and my business in a whole new way.

When I see people become first-time authors and they hold that first book, the smile cannot be wiped off their face. They always say to me, 'Nat, I'm so glad you made me do this, you've changed my life.' How would you feel if people came up to you, having read your book or whatever way you have helped them, and they say, 'You changed my life, I cannot thank you enough'?

That is ultimately what people want to do at a certain time in our lives. Being financially rewarded by your business is one thing that provides lifestyle and pays the bills, but what truly rewards a human being is being able to make a difference to another. This is the level of contribution where it's good for your client, good for you, and provides a greater good.

Sometimes people can be concerned about the financial side of investing in the process of writing their first book, but what they fail to see, having been through this journey so many times with so many people, it is actually at the other end of them holding that book where they're going to be a new person.

If you're a parent or you've had a major life change, you would agree that you had an identity shift when you became a parent, or you have had certain things change drastically in your life. It is that shift that I see happen when someone receives their first book. It turns them into a different human being who thinks about themselves differently, who sees the world from a slightly different perspective. It is this personal transformation that creates the life and business transformation beyond the book coming out.

Writing your first book is not about the book; it's about the person you become at the other end of it. It is a very powerful quote, and I wish more people could truly understand the enormity in what it actually means. Give yourself the gift of this positive transformation, because it is an identity shift that can set you up for life in so many ways.

44. ULTIMATE BOOK MARKETING

Your book is your business card on steroids. Whether you like it or not, your book is going to make you more visible with the message you share, the problem that you solve, and how further people can engage with you in more depth. Don't waste valuable real estate space that exists within your book when it comes to further promoting and marketing your business.

This chapter is for those of you who are writing your first book because you want to grow your business, and to help even more people. I have a few little tips, but for more depth on this topic, in *Ultimate 48 Hour Author* I share lots more around leveraging and marketing your book, and how to utilise your book to generate leads.

Have an offer in your book that is going to invite people to get some kind of additional bonus. An example, using this book, would be for you to go and grab yourself a free full eBook version of *Ultimate 48 Hour Author*. You can get that at www.ultimate48hourauthor.com. au/gift. I have got a landing page set up where you can download your book, and that's where you will put in your name, email, and contact number, and that book will come to you electronically.

What this will then do is enable us to continue the conversation, in terms of how further we can help you to write your book. We aim to send out extra content that adds value, with tips and tricks to get your book written. We don't hold back; we literally give people as much as possible to make their decision, or perhaps to just simply empower them do it by themselves.

Other things you should consider, if you do want to be a speaker, is to add your speaker bio at the back of the book, and have other programs, like online courses that you might want to advertise. Once someone has read your book and loved your content, they may want to go deeper in the information that you have shared. Why not have a way for them to connect with you, reach out to you, and ask you further about the ways they can get support from you?

Remember, sometimes people don't read your whole book, so a little tip here is to put your lead magnet, or call to action in your first chapter, somewhere it can logically appear. If people only download a sample of your book off Amazon, or other platforms that give away a sample, then you can still have that opportunity to engage with that person. If they have loved what they've read in the sample and downloaded the bonus, they'll continue being on your email subscription list to receive a lot more valuable tips from you.

Make sure that all your contact details are spelled correctly and that people can easily reach you.

45. INTANGIBLE MAGIC

As I have said a few times, your book is your business card on steroids. It is going to increase your credibility in the eyes of others. It is still very rare and unique when you look at the amount of people who actually back themselves into becoming authors. This is the whole reason why I'm writing this book; I want more people to back themselves and write their first book, which means more of the human knowledge that exists around our world can be shared. We can be learning a lot more and evolving to the next stage of human evolution.

Credibility is the big factor that comes to those people who are writing this for business purposes, because it also enables you to further grow your business, you are likely to get more clients, more leads, and will be easily referred to because you have got your tool, which is your book.

Credibility is one of the aspects that every person in business needs to look at, even on a personal level. Do you have a website, and how are you promoting yourself? The three rock star profile aspects are being featured as an author, a speaker, and a person in the media. We should always be promoting these key things as aspects of what we do and how we do it, because when people see those three things, they believe we are more of an expert. By putting ourselves out there in these three different ways – by writing a book, by speaking live in front of audiences, and by being in the media – it means that there has to be some expertise and integrity behind our message, as we are doing it publicly.

They can see that we're not hiding behind closed doors just coaching, or speaking to people one-on-one, but that we actually have backed ourselves in with our message and the system that we're delivering, and that we are sharing this on a wider scale.

If you do have a website, make sure your book is splattered all over every page. Make sure you put all your media logos if you have appeared in the media, and if you haven't, look to do that once your book does come out. Do some speaking, if that is one of your goals. Put yourself out there, and put your hand up to present at speaking events.

Credibility is one thing that was lacking in my own business when I started out, and the whole idea behind me writing my first book was actually to develop and build that, over having a personal bucket list desire of writing my book.

Everyone's reason for writing their first book is different. Some people do it as a healing journey, some people do it for themselves as a credibility and marketing tool, other people do it because it's therapeutic, a few do it because they want to tell their life story to leave it as that legacy for their family. Whatever reason you have is okay. If you are a business owner and you are looking for the book to support your business, then credibility is one of the things you can look forward to once you have your book in hands.

46. DECLARE YOU ARE THE EXPERT

How does one become an expert? I used to think that you had to have some special doctorate degree, and that someone else had to declare you to be the expert. Then I wrote a book. All of a sudden people started inviting me to speak at their health and wellness centers, chiropractor clinics, personal training studios, and they were presenting me as being the expert.

I thought, *Oh, my goodness!* I needed to position myself as an expert and say, 'You know what, I am the expert in this because I'm passionate about this topic. I've learnt it in a lot more detail than anyone else I know, and therefore I declare that I'm the expert.'

That's been my journey. Certainly, other people have done it in a reverse order, whereby they have done so much work with so many clients, and they have so many testimonials that they become the go-to expert, then they write their book on their expertise.

My journey and experience in this has been to position myself and bring out my expertise in a book, announce myself as the expert, and then have others buy into that. That lead to others inviting me to speak at certain events, which evolved into me working with more clients and developing my system further. This eventuated into a licensed model, my weight-loss book was converted into a licensed system, I was selling my intellectual property so other coaches and health and wellness practitioners could work with my mindset program, and my brand kept growing.

Once I established the expert status, I started to see the need for me to set up my personal brand. I've set up a personal branding website (www.NatasaDenman.com) where I display all the credibility around the things that I've done, things that I've got coming up, the books that I've written, the books that I've helped people write with us, and, of course, the way people can contact me.

Nowadays, not only am I being invited to speak on my expertise, which is writing your first book in 48 hours, but also on my personal brand and the success I've had. I speak a lot on being a 'mumpreneur', because I had two of my children during the middle of getting my business off the ground. We've raised three little babies whilst on this entrepreneurial journey, and they're still very little – at the time of writing this book, they're just three, six, and nine.

My personal brand, and your personal brand, is something to seriously think about because if anything else happens and your current business model fails or implodes, the one thing that can never disappear is your reputation and your personal brand.

So, it is time to embrace it, make sure you buy your full name domain. It's time to look in the future and develop your own personal branding site. You never know; if people see you as the expert on something specific, you'll then be able to get opportunities to speak on certain topics, and maybe even be flown all around the world to share your passion with big organisations and groups. It's just one of the benefits of writing that first book and declaring that you are the expert.

47. SELL WITH STYLE AND GRACE

If you're writing a book for the purposes of wanting people to progress into a different area of your business like coaching, consulting, online programs, retreats, or other ways of learning further from you, it is important that people know that these kinds of things do exist.

There are more blatant ways of doing it, meaning that you would place your offers or your next steps at the back of the book, as I discussed earlier, but there are also subtle ways where you can naturally mention the things that you have going on in your business throughout the content of your book. That is what we call 'seeding'.

Seeding is selling without selling. It's letting people know what you do on a regular basis with clients, and how you interact with people in your business, without saying what you do. An example of this has been throughout this book; I've often mentioned my retreats, the *Ultimate 48 Hour Author* books, and some other books that I've written. I have mentioned my half-day workshop and event, my signature way to get people to know us on a deeper level. From hearing that, some of you may decide, 'Hey, I want to check out what this half-day event is, or find out a little bit more.'

I did a similar thing when my husband and I were writing *Guilt Free Parents*. That particular book was not written to have any further support in terms of parenting coaching, or helping people with their challenges while building a business and raising very small children. Throughout the book I naturally talked about the style of business that we run, and the fact that we do our *Ultimate 48 Hour Author* retreats, and mentioned that as part of the content. I was seeding, on some level, what our business is about. If those mums or dads in business who were reading the book were looking to write their own book, they would have been curious and interested in checking us out, and seeing if we would be a match for them to work with.

It's really important to think how is it that you're going to mention it throughout your content. You're not to be pitchy and really obvious; it needs to feel natural, inserted when you're sharing about what you do, and the things you've heard and experienced throughout your work. That's why we have featured some of our authors at the back of this book; their stories as they embarked on writing their very first book. In a way, it is showcasing what we also do, but adding value at the same time.

When you think about seeding, it happens because you want to add further value, not so much promote your business, whereas the offers at the back of the book and the lead magnet from the start of your book are more blatant calls to action.

48. LEVERAGE IS THE GAME-CHANGER

When I meet wannabe first-time authors, they always ask, 'How many books should I anticipate selling, or how many books has your most famous author sold?' And the answer is really, 'I don't know!'

This is because our focus at Ultimate 48 Hour Author is in what we do and how we help people, not about book sales. As I said previously, every different organisation or company that teaches people to write books is going to have a different intention for the outcome they aim to achieve with that particular author.

Traditional publishing houses will aim more at book sales and a high volume of books. Other organisations might position themselves and really pay attention to that bestseller status that they want to execute for you. With us, it's about leverage. We really want the return on investment, not to come from a volume of book sales, because to sell $100,000 worth of books is a long, hard, and very time-consuming endeavor.

To sell $100,000 worth of books:

- you have to be in the top 2% of published authors in your country.

- you will need to be in every major book store in the country, who takes more than 70% of the cost of the sale, leaving very little for you. Imagine how many units needs to be sold to make six figures.

- you will need to spend most of your waking hours promoting, spruiking, and pushing your book.

- ... actually, it would be easier to just go and get a job, but with the average wage in Australia around $50K, well, you better go and get two jobs!

The focus is that the return on investment should come from people engaging your services and further training that you offer beyond the books content. I've always said that books are just knowledge and information; they're a great rapport and relationship-building tool, your business card on steroids, but the transformation that you can provide for people will happen more through hand-holding. It will happen through having online programs, coaching, and educational material that you can give people with more depth behind the information you share within your book.

I believe the focus should always be on where will this book get my foot in the door? Will it be to get more media opportunities, to pick up more speaking gigs? Develop further programs and intellectual property from this base content, then you only need to sign up 4-5 consulting clients, or sell 10 online programs, rather than 2,000 books to cover your investment in publishing your book.

Return on investment with books should be looked at in regards to what is happening beyond the release of the book. Where are people going, and how is this set up in your business? This is where that outsider's expert view of your topic is essential, because they can see that future and keep in mind where you want to end up, rather than focusing on volume of books.

PART 4

First-time Author Insights

FIRST-TIME AUTHOR INSIGHTS

When I asked my authors if they would like to be part of this book, I was looking for 10 interviews. I got more than 40.

I was really torn about which to select and which to leave out; they all had so much gold and wisdom. So, the way I selected them was on variety of niches, types of books, and different obstacles that were holding them back so that I could illustrate the usefulness of the 48 mini-chapters I have delivered to you in this book. I wanted you to hear it from the horse's mouth, as they say, and for those who did not make it in the book, please go ahead and download the electronic PDF version that contains the rest:

http://bit.ly/shutupfreeebook

Let's get started ...

AMANDA AKERS

Author of *Frozen Families: 7 Essentials for Survival When You Have an Ice User in Your Life*

What is your book about and why did you write it?

Frozen Families is a book that came together as a result of my work as a Clinical Psychologist, specializing in the field of drugs and alcohol. My university studies, including drug and alcohol research, enabled me to work in the public and private sector of the drug and alcohol field in NSW.

My book also came about as a result of life experiences that I have battled over the years, and tend not to disclose to others. During my first marriage, in my early 20s, my husband became a drug user after the birth of our first child, and despite 10 years of supporting him through rehabs and other recovery options, I was unable to continue to live with his behaviour. I eventually left the marriage, only to be shunned by my in-laws for failing to stay with my drug-using husband 'til death us do part. I have never regretted my decision, it took a long time to decide, but that was many years ago. It kindled an ongoing interest in the drug and alcohol field for me, though, as so many questions were left unanswered. For example, would a person make such a decision to cease contact if it was their child?

More recently, one of my adult children from my first marriage, along with several of his friends, engaged in the use of methamphetamine. Commonly known as 'ice', this caused even more severe disruptions to my life. My extended family had never held high hopes for my son, given that his father had been a drug user, and they provided little support while my son grew up not knowing his biological father, causing me to keep my recent experiences with my son's ice use to myself.

As a Clinical Psychologist I have supported clients, as well as their families, to manage ice abuse and its consequences, and I found myself teaching families the same skills time and time again during their therapy sessions. I have discussed professional and personal issues relating to ice use with my supervisors during my career and I was acutely aware of the theoretical concepts I was required to utilize. I continued to have a desire to help families, clients, and non-clients to manage the manipulations and abuse that they experienced when communicating with family members using ice, while I practiced using these skills myself.

The *Frozen Families* book developed as a way to put these skills into writing in an easy-to-read self-help book that family members could read in the privacy of their own home. It would enable them to discuss and manage aspects of their lives without feeling they were doing it alone. Frozen Families opens up the conversation about having an ice user in your life with some of the basic psychological concepts used in therapy.

What was your biggest challenge in deciding to write your first book?

My biggest challenge in deciding to write my first book was the idea of *facing my own shame*. This included a fear that readers would automatically assume that I had an ice user in my life. Of course, they'd be right, but that's not my story to tell, so I don't tell it. As a result, I had to work out how to weave stories into my book that were not my family stories, and were not my clients' stories, but were typical stories based on factual cases, some of which I had

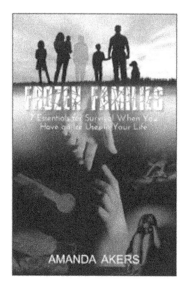

experienced firsthand. I had to dare to tell them. I also had to keep building my new private practice and I *couldn't afford to take much time off work* to write a book.

Admittedly, I had some aspects of denial about my adult son's drug use as well, and by putting the lessons I'd learned into writing, based on psychological knowledge, *it helped reduce my denial and enhance my acceptance*, as well as my knowledge about ice use, treatments, and the possibility of successful recovery. I wanted to find and express hope and share that hope with others.

Who were your biggest doubters and has their opinion changed now that you are published?

While I was writing my book, I didn't come across any doubters, basically because *I hadn't told many people that I was writing a book.* I wanted to write it and present it to the world with no prior negativity. I believed in it. I knew this book had to be written for others, and for myself. I've had firsthand experience of being treated differently, even though I don't use drugs. *My own family, with the exception of my oldest brother, had been doubters for many years* since my first marriage, despite my subsequent career success and partner choices. I wanted to avoid doubters and focus on positivity while I was writing. I planned to share optimism on the backdrop of the stark reality of the long, horrid ride that families can experience, sometimes alone, when their child or partner is using ice.

Why did you decide to do the Ultimate 48 Hour Author Program for your first book?

I first heard Natasa Denman speak at a networking event at the Gold Coast. Natasa spoke with clarity and confidence as she presented the Ultimate 48 Hour Author program in just 5 minutes!

I walked away with Natasa's words in my head and it confirmed for me that writing a book was a good way to get the message out. I wanted to write it as quickly as possible. I wanted to write about ice, and I feared that if I left it too long there'd be a new drug on the scene by the time I'd written a book. Without help, I knew it'd take me two to three years to write and publish a book. After hearing Natasa speak, I followed her on social media and soon saw she was running a half-day workshop at the Gold Coast. I quickly booked in. I knew before I attended the half-day workshop that I was very interested in signing up for the Ultimate 48 Hour Author Retreat to write my book. I wanted to do this!

My main barrier was the cost. I'd just relocated from NSW and I was building my new private practice at the Gold Coast, which felt like starting my career all over again, and I wasn't earning a lot. But I was determined! During Natasa's half-day workshop she mentioned a payment plan, and that was it – I was in! And it was only going to require two days away from work to attend the retreat. My mind was truly made up, I was totally convinced! It was a smooth ride for me from that day onwards.

What is your best piece of advice you can share with a first-time author?

My advice to first time authors is: ***don't leave it until it's too late***. Write your book now. Don't spend time trying to sort out how to get a book written and published. Use information that is already tried and tested. The Ultimate 48 Hour Author package is complete, it's all ready for you to jump right in, write your book, and have it published in a short timeframe. On this journey you'll meet lifelong friends who will support you and encourage you. You'll never look back. I know I haven't.

What has happened now that your first book is out?
While I was writing *Frozen Families* at the Ultimate 48 Hour Author Retreat, I was invited to do a radio interview. I hadn't even written my book yet! Since publishing, I've had **organizations purchase multiple copies of my book** to give to their psychologists and counsellors, and even their board members. I've been **invited to speak at retreats and workshops**, and drug and alcohol workers' training programs. Whilst I haven't become a celebrity, that was never my plan. I'm a psychologist, I provide therapy. My goal was to engage people in the conversation about the impact of ice use on families and to help people reduce the stress in their lives. Since writing my book I've had people tell me I'm brave for writing on such a topic. I've had people thank me profusely. **My clients love the fact I've written a book** as it confirms that I have expertise in this difficult area. My private practice is successful, as I've **improved my credibility** in a new region where I was previously unknown. **The orders for my book keep coming in!**

On a personal level, I found the process of writing this book to be therapeutic. It helped my own family, as two of my adult children learned a lot from reading and contributing to the process of writing the book. It gave me a focus while life was challenging. I now feel stronger in my resolve and knowledge, and most importantly, once again, I have a positive relationship with my oldest son who, at the time of writing this information, is not using ice. My last chapter came true!

Will you be writing more books in the future?
With the success of *Frozen Families*, I'm planning to write a second book, one that compliments my first book. Frozen Families provides strategies on how to manage the family member using ice. The

ongoing struggle involves helping the family member using ice to gain external assistance, such as rehabilitation. The *Frozen Families* sequel is on its way!

To purchase Amanda's book:
www.facebook.com/FrozenFamilies/

ANITA BENTATA

Author of *The Wolf in a Suit – The 7 Secrets Inside Relationship Abuse, Fairytales and Truths for Women, Community and Professionals*

What is your book about and why did you write it?
I wrote *The Wolf in a Suit* because of a promise I made in 1996. I ran a women's domestic violence survivors group. They asked me to write a book and explain why women stay with their partners.

My book does far more than this, as I explore the understandings from my perspective as a survivor and professional psychotherapist of 23 years, trained in trauma and abuse. I incorporate 11 original reinterpreted fairy tales and information that is still not common knowledge.

I wanted my book to become the domestic violence manual for women; the guide my younger self needed when I first went out into the world, so naive and ill-equipped. I wanted this book to educate 'normal' families about talking about the uncomfortable, and how to provide support to those they say they love. I wanted to change the system so children like mine could be better protected and supported. I wanted to pass on my knowledge before I retire.

What was your biggest challenge in deciding to write your first book?
I knew there were **family members on both sides who wouldn't like me telling my story**. I wrote a very detailed, uncensored account of family and relationship life, and I knew it would trigger their buttons and picture of reality.

My book is a lot larger than your typical book, so staying on track was important. Each chapter was clear and coherent for the reader. Natasa's chaired guide was very helpful.

I was slightly **concerned I could be sued**, but on hearing about past authors experiences, support from my new 'family' in our Ultimate 48 Hour Author weekend team, and my own research, I found I was pretty safe; given I'm telling the truth, and my intention was to educate, not to publicly identify or shame anyone.

Who were your biggest doubters, and has their opinion changed now that you are published?
Some family members didn't want me to write the book. After **receiving threats and emotional bullying** there seems to be a greater acceptance that I will not be silenced in speaking my story. They have since begun some changes in attitudes, memories, and decisions since publishing my book.

Why did you decide to do the Ultimate 48 Hour Author Program for your first book?
I love Natasa; her genuineness, clarity, organisational skills, and her down to Earth realness. I knew I had achieved a lot on my own, but to go up a level I was overdue in receiving the support and guidance in areas out of my expertise.

What is your best piece of advice you can share with a first-time author?
Stick to Natasa's expert guidance (my amazing book cover design is due to Natasa's idea) with the freedom to adjust what you need to do to maintain your unique heart message.

Dream big enough that it's uncomfortable, then go for it! This is only the beginning! What you imagine now is just the first step. Like a piece of clay, you may have an initial idea, but the clay will shape you beyond your conscious dream, and will continue to unfold to its possibilities! Surrender!

What has happened now that you first book is out?
I have written four more books with about 10 more planned! I have more products in the works. I am a key interviewee and Executive Producer of the documentary *Dangerous Dance*, to be released in 2018. I have spoken nationally at conferences. I have had skilled professionals wanting to support my mission. I have made links with key people in the field, and made important relationships based on my book. I have met some amazing famous people, and had people with 90,000+ followers want to support and collaborate in business opportunities.

My confidence has expanded to lift the lid on what I want my business to transform into. My confidence has enabled me to initiate and ask for support from key leaders and influencers. I tour Australia speaking to women, with repeated requests to return. I have launched an online five and 10-week program for women and professionals, as well as developed a volunteer program for women to support other women. I am launching an exciting new affordable online membership site in 2018 to support all women impacted by childhood or adult domestic violence, especially those who can't afford specialised trauma and abuse therapy. I run groups for women survivors, now with over 700 women!

To purchase Anita's book:
www.anitabentata.com

DONNA REESE

Author of *Don't Tell Me I Can't*

What is your book about and why did you write it?
For the better part of my adult life, I've had many people tell me that I needed to write a book. Things that have happened for me, and to me, are often hard to believe. From a young age, I've been faced many times with people who either didn't believe in me, or simply told me that I couldn't do what I was setting out to do. When I look back, I think my attitude was attracting the wrong type of people into my life. I was negative, so how could I expect a positive outcome?

When I was told I couldn't do something, I set out on a mission to accomplish it for all the wrong reasons – to prove people wrong. When I started reaching my goals, my confidence grew and my attitude changed. I was attracting good things and people. By age 29 I was buying a second business and was living a life that my friends were only dreaming about.

As life would have it, I hit a major roadblock at age 37 when I was diagnosed with degenerative disc disease. This was during the time period when I had also just filed for divorce from my business partner, and father of my two sons. I kept pushing forward, setting lofty goals while working through a disease that would eventually overwhelm me.

I wrote the book to share some of my stories that I hope will inspire anyone who reads it to realize that anything you set your mind to is possible, even with incredible adversity.

What was your biggest challenge in deciding to write your first book?
The biggest challenge for me was timing. When I was running my businesses and serving my community in a publicly-elected position on the school board, time was something that was a commodity. Sadly, my health was on the decline and I was told by two neurosurgeons that my life was essentially over at the age of 49. Now I had all the time in the world, but I was struggling through debilitating pain daily. ***Trying to find focus through the pain*** was the number one challenge that I've been faced with throughout my lifetime.

Who were your biggest doubters and has their opinion changed now that you are published?
I think my biggest doubter was not only my best friend, but also ***my current housemate,*** living with me to help tend to my medical needs. He had worked for me when I was an active entrepreneur, but now he saw me struggle to get out of bed each day. I kept talking about writing, even enlisting his talent as a writer to assist me. Each time I brought it up, I got the doubtful nod of his head. In hindsight, it's disheartening to realize that someone who was once my biggest cheerleader had lost faith in me. I now feel as if I was a bit abandoned during a time that I needed emotional support more than ever.

I went ahead and started writing on April 4 2017. Fast forward a year later, I gave up asking for his help, and announced on April 3 (nearly one year to the date of typing my first word), that my book was going to be in my hand by September. His simple response was, 'I am so proud of you.' I think now that he may be the one holding the most regret because I persevered, even during a time that he didn't believe in me.

Why did you decide to do the Ultimate 48 Hour Author Program for your first book?
I had met many first-time authors while earning my public speaking certification with world renowned motivational speaker, Les Brown. Les himself is a multiple bestselling author. Writing wasn't my problem, but organizing and the research I did on how to publish it was more than overwhelming. I had put publishing my book in my 10X planner for a goal that I wanted to achieve within 60 days. That was at the end of February 2018. On April 3 I attended the seminar out of pure curiosity. That showed me how I could reach my goal before my 60 day projection date!

In my book I dedicated an entire chapter to the importance of having good mentors. I could have wasted a lot of time and money trying to figure out something that was now right at the tips of my fingers. No matter what point you are in life, enlisting the expertise of those who have 'been there and done that' is the best decision you can make when wanting to reach your goals at a much more rapid pace. I literally could still be doing research on Google and Amazon, hoping to figure it out, but instead I'm planning a book launch party with 100 of my closest friends for this fall!

What advice would you give a first-time author?
The advice I would give to a first-time author is that *if you lived what you are writing about, your end product will be much more powerful to the reader.* For instance, don't write a book on effective

parenting if you are not a parent. I read books to keep me inspired and on track. The author's credibility and experiences related to their writing is what I look for when choosing to purchase a book.

What has happened now that your first book is out?
The book is in the publication mode, yet I am already using it to **launch a new career** at the age of 53 as a motivational speaker and entrepreneurial coach. The **confidence that I have when selling myself to potential clients increased dramatically,** being able to show credibility as an author. Not only are people wanting to buy my book, they suddenly want to buy me and my message.

Will you be writing more books in the future?
I truly believe this will be the first of many books. My first book sums up how I achieved success through adversity and tenacity. In writing it, I realized that there are many individual stories that can help improve the lives of others. At a recent training I spoke about balance of being a single mother and entrepreneur. When I was finished I had a father ask me if I had ever written a book about what I just spoke on. He told me, 'If you haven't, I recommend that you do.'

Another area that, sadly, I have too much experience with is tragic loss. In 2017 I lost two sisters unexpectedly within four months of one another. This was a few short years after losing a nephew to suicide. I had to pull myself out of a deep depression and the negative mindset that could have changed the direction of my life. I have so much that I am passionate about, and real life stories are those that sell best!

To purchase Donnas book:
www.donnaraeinspires.com

FRANCESCA MOI

Author of *Follow Me!*

What is your book about and why did you write it?
My book is about helping people grow their network so they can BOOM their business, as I have done for myself! I grew a six-figure business in just eight months, and if an Italian girl who started with no friends or family in Australia could do this, anyone could! I know the importance of growing a following and running live events, and in my book I was able to create easy,  actionable steps, and real-life examples for entrepreneurs at any stage of the business journey!

I wrote my book because a lot of people were messaging me on Facebook asking for a quick solution for building a network, and I couldn't explain in two words what they had to do. The book includes online and offline strategies on how people can BOOM their business by becoming people of influence, and step up as a leader in their community.

The book is great as Natasa teaches us how to speak out the book. I get feedback from people that the book is so easy to read and they hear my voice while they read it. Great to build trust with my raving fans!

What was your biggest challenge in deciding to write your first book?
I didn't know where to start. I wondered if people would really want to read a book written by a foreigner. I wondered, *'Am I good*

enough?' All of these limiting beliefs came to mind before I wrote my book, and during the writing process. I never thought I was going to be an author and the process of writing a book scared me... it was put in the too-hard basket.

Who were your biggest doubters and has their opinion changed now that you are published?
I didn't really have any doubters, but it all happened so fast! I told people I was writing a book, and 10 days later I was at the retreat! I think people didn't expect me to have a book finished in just four months.

Why did you decide to do the Ultimate 48 Hour Author Program for your first book?
Because I am an activator and not famous for completing things! I knew that the Ultimate 48 Hour Author program would be a kick in the butt to get it done and get it out there.

When I attended Natasa's half-day workshop I realised that I needed a book to take my business to the next level, and to show people I was serious about my business and that I was an expert in my niche. Natasa made it sound so easy and fun, and I was in!

I cannot think of anything worse than sitting down to write for hours ... her method of speaking the book out is fun, fast, and it's a no brainer. I went to a luxurious weekend and BOOM my book was DONE!

I couldn't have done it any other way. I'm about to write my third book with them!

What is your best piece of advice you can share with a first-time author?

Don't even think about doing it yourself! Just go to Ultimate 48 Hour Author and it will be done in no time! From unpacking the idea of your book, to editing, to the cover, to the title, to printing, they take care of ALL of that for you! It's a no-brainer!

The first thing I would advise is that you have a book in you, if you have had clients in the past, and you know you are an expert. Don't wait until all the ducks align because they will align only when you have taken action and back yourself up by believing you have a book in you.

What has happened now that your first book is out?

After my first book was out, *my credibility and status went up.* Now people introduce me as an author, and straight away people have more respect for me and are willing to listen. I have more confidence, as I now have a book to back me up. It's a great present to give to workshop attendees, and it helps me with sales. Like Natasa says, it's a business card on steroids!

The book is literally being repurposed in thousands of ways from my team. They use it to write blogs for me, and they use it to create opt-in so we can get emails from my raving fans by giving away the eBook version, or the first chapter. It works like magic.

I have to just say to my team to get the content from the book and BOOM, they use it to create newsletters and websites and power points. It's fabulous that all my content is in the book and I don't have to keep writing about it ... all we need to do is repurpose it.

When people buy my half day workshop we have always included in a package a signed copy of my book. When I speak at events I have created a bundle with the book and other products. This way people get something tangible, and they love it! I am using the book for corporate gigs and adding it to value pack for attendees.

The book has helped me with some revenue, too, at each workshop we sell between $100 and $300 in books. It is great to cover part of the costs of running the event.

When people come to my workshop they have already spent 3-4 hours reading my book so they feel they already know me, and it's great for building trust and helps them to making a faster decision if they want to work with me.

At the speaking gigs I always give away a book so I get a chance to talk about my books again, as the organiser has already introduced me as an author.

Will you be writing more books in the future?
I already wrote my second one, *Bums on Seats*, and I am about to start my third one soon!

To purchase Francesca's book:
www.empoweringevents.com.au/books/

JAMES BOMFORD

Author of What the F#K is The Cloud?*

What is your book about and why did you write it?

The book is about cloud computing and how businesses can benefit from moving their systems into the cloud. It gives business owners some tips and tricks around securing their business and making sure that their data is safe, the pitfalls to look out for, and where money can be made and saved.

I had a lot of questions from clients – it happens a lot when running an IT company – and the questions were usually the same; revolving around security, safety, and privacy. So, I decided to write a book and use it as a marketing tool, but also as a self-help tool for those businesses deciding whether or not they want to move to cloud computing or not.

What was your biggest challenge in deciding to write your first book?

The biggest challenge when I decided to write the book was *the structure* and what to write about specifically. It was quite a challenge knowing I had all this knowledge in my head, but how would I segment it into chapters that flow and appear coherent and in a way that people can relate to and understand without heap of geek speak.

Who were your biggest doubters and has their opinion changed now that you are published?

I didn't really have any doubters; most people were excited and wanted to know more about the book and why I decided to write one. There was no one who really didn't like the idea of me writing a book, mainly because it was one of those spur-of-the-moment things when I was attending a course that Natasa was running. It certainly was an epiphany that I could do some great things when I wrote a book that would benefit so many people, and help them get their businesses out of the digital darkness.

Why did you decide to do the Ultimate 48 Hour Author Program for your first book?

I decided to do the Ultimate 48 Hour Author program after I attended a seminar that Natasa ran. At the time I actually attended with thoughts of supporting a friend, but ended up staying because the information and ideas from a business point of view were so good, and made so much sense when it came to taking my business to the next level. Taking all that I know and putting it down on paper and giving it to people as a book was not only a great way to share my knowledge in assisting business owners, it was an excellent marketing tool for the business and my own personal branding, too.

What is your best piece of advice you can share with a first-time author?

The best piece of advice I would share with a first-time author is to **understand that there are systems and support**. Starting a project like this is daunting as there are so many pieces of the puzzle to come together, but having the system in place that takes you from an idea in your head all the way through the process to a completed printed book takes all the stress and potential hurdles away completely.

Having the support of people who have done the process helps keep your mind at ease and means things are done far quicker and easier than you think possible when publishing a book. Coming from an IT background means I love systems; they help put things in the correct place and in the right order. The system that was set up and designed for writing a book enables you to take all the thoughts that are rushing around everywhere in your head and actually put them down in a structured, coherent manner that flows and enables you to really get that book written, but get it written in a way that is really understandable and readable.

What has happened now that your first book is out?
Since the book has been out I've had **great interest from some of the big players.** Our company has **partnered with the likes of Dropbox, Trend Micro, Microsoft,** and a couple of others who really like the information that I'm putting forward; they want to be able to convey it to their clients in a way that businesses owners understand. Being published has also enabled me to present as a **keynote speaker at many events,** enabling me to be able to share my message as well as **get new clients** and being able to move them to new cloud-based systems.

Will you be writing more books in the future?
I probably will write another book. There's certainly a huge amount of knowledge that I have gained while running a business, especially when it comes to cloud computing. I don't think it will be so much in the technology space, as the focus will be more on business systems and how streamlined and lean a business can run when

both business systems and technology systems fit together. Because technology has changed, businesses can run at a much faster pace with fewer employees; even writing a book can be done in a few short hours thanks to changes and developments in technology bringing the world closer together.

To purchase James's book:
www.rightclickit.com.au

KAREN SINGERY

Author of *After the Shock – How to Make Peace with Change*

What is your book about and why did you write it?
My book *After the Shock* is about helping people to navigate through change peacefully. This book is for people who want a smoother transition through change, to smash all the negativity, and to ultimately reach a place of acceptance, peace and love. Very often CHANGE will rock the foundation of your world. It will have you feeling confused, anxious, and depressed. For some, unfortunately, they eventually give up.

You know where you want to be in your life but you have no clue how to get there. You are constantly searching for ways to navigate yourself through this pain that you are experiencing, but you feel lost.

I decided to write this book with a purpose, to help answer the questions I'm often asked, 'How do you do it? You have been through so much change, yet you are able to pick yourself up, embrace it, and always look for the gift in it.'

I didn't always embrace change. As a child, I despised it. The word 'change' was a swear word to me. It meant moving out of my comfort zone. It meant starting anew. It meant going through pain that I didn't want to feel or face. Facing them head-on were the most challenging things for me.

Did I have a choice with the many changes I went through? No! But I soon realised that I did have a choice as to how I was going to respond to those events that changed the course of my life.

We all have a story within us that needs to come out in some way or another. My change is no different or worse than anyone else's, and I thought that if I could support and help someone through my book to handle change a lot better, then I have given back to the world.

The second reason for writing my book was two-fold. It was to use it as a manual for my workshops so that people could have something tangible to read and to work from, and it is a great marketing tool to be able to say that you are a published author. It most definitely gives you credibility.

What was your biggest challenge in deciding to write your first book?

The biggest challenge for me was ***the content. How was I going to organise it,*** and what was I going to include in my book? I had ***no idea where and how to begin.*** What was the structure of the book going to look like, and who was going to be my target market? Fortunately I had already heard about Natasa's program through the coaching circles I frequented. It was a no-brainer to approach her for help.

Who were your biggest doubters and has their opinion changed now that you are published?
I was very fortunate in that I never had any doubters. I only ever experienced immense support and encouragement. ***My biggest doubter was me.*** I always felt that I couldn't do this as I had always been made to believe that my written English wasn't good. The meaning I gave this was that I would never be good at putting pen to paper. How wrong they were. As I immersed myself into writing my book I realised nothing is going to hold me back. Now I have an amazing book that not only looks good, but has amazing content that is easy to read.

People I have spoken to, and ***my family and friends are absolutely amazed*** that I have written a book, and even more so in ***only four months***.

Why did you decide to do the Ultimate 48 Hour Author Program for your first book?
For me, the Ultimate 48 Hour Author Program is so slick and easy to do. Today people are looking for solutions that are simple to follow. The variety of support provided is endless; like having Natasa's and Stuart's astounding knowledge on tap, your publisher is sorted out for you, an editor is selected for you. Richard transcribes your book, Kevin does a photographic shoot with you, and Nikola can help you with your diagrams, book cover, etc. Oh my word, the support is amazing.

There is even more … you can attend Unlimited 2 Day face-to-face masterclasses (which run 4 times a year) to support you with marketing your book. The Ultimate 48 Hour Author Program has your back at all times. Natasa and her team want to see you succeed, and the assistance is immeasurable.

114

What is your best piece of advice you can share with a first-time author?

Just do it, trust yourself and the process that Natasa offers. Set yourself daily mini-goals, and before you know it, your book will be done and dusted. I completed mine in just four months. Something I didn't do was practice recording a few chapters before the weekend. I would strongly recommend that you do this to get comfortable with recording yourself. This will help to speed up the process even more. *Get over yourself and your self-doubt*, use them as motivators to get your book out there. You've got this!

What has happened now that your first book is out?

I have had numerous *speaking gigs* where I have sold my book. I *hosted my own radio show,* and interviewed some amazing authors, one being Natasa. I have been interviewed on the radio. I co-authored in another book, and am currently writing an eBook for an organisation that helps teenagers with personal development. I have contributed towards an eBook for a naturopath. I cannot wait to see what's next to come.

Will you be writing more books in the future?

Most definitely. I have a book for teens in the pipeline. It's still in my head, and as soon as I have completed my eBook for teens, this will be my next project. The sky is the limit.

Link to Karen's website to purchase her book –
www.pathwaysunlimited.com.au

KYM DEGENHART

Author of *Frou Frou to Fruition*

What is your book about and why did you write it?
In Frou Frou to Fruition I share my experiences as a professional dancer, dance teacher, and dance studio owner to deliver insider tips, helping those who love to dance find success in the dance industry. I couldn't imagine my life without dance; the places it has taken me, the experiences I have gained, and the people I have met.

I started dancing when I was six, and have never stopped. I landed a position as a cancan dancer at the Moulin Rouge in Paris at 21, and continued to dance professionally for 10 years before returning to teach dance. I was teaching in government schools when given the opportunity to purchase Bom Funk Dance Studio, and take over as Principal and Director. The challenges of running a small business provided a steep learning curve, but thanks to my past experience and my willingness to learn, Bom Funk has continued to grow from strength to strength, and is now a thriving six-figure business.

People are quick to dismiss dance as a legitimate career path, but there are so many opportunities to connect with others and to create meaningful work in this industry. There is also the bonus of being able to work in an area I am so passionate about. My book delves deep into many of the challenges that dancers, dance teachers, and studio owners face, and provides actionable steps to overcome these and succeed. My greatest wish is to inspire and assist others to follow their dreams and continue their dance journey.

What was your biggest challenge in deciding to write your first book?

My biggest challenge in deciding to write a book was *self-doubt*. I struggled with the notion of being an expert in my field, and wasn't sure anyone would be interested in my advice. I saw authors as highly prestigious professionals, and I looked at other leaders in this industry as being so much more experienced than myself.

It took me some time to realise that I was already providing so much advice and expertise to others in the dance industry, particularly because my journey had touched on so many roles with my performing, teaching, journalism, events, and business experience. Gradually, I learned to change my mindset around this, as I realised that I did have insights worthy of sharing, particularly if it helped others and helped improve standards. I was lucky to have a number of close family, friends, colleagues, and mentors continuously encourage me and help me truly believe in myself.

Who were your biggest doubters and has their opinion changed now that you are published?

Some of my family doubted the concept of writing a book in 48 hours and voiced that they couldn't imagine following the formula themselves, but they never doubted me personally achieving my goal. My close friends and family know that when I set my mind to something, I make it happen through sheer determination, and more than a little stubbornness. I also surround myself with supporters and positive mentors, so if there were doubters, I didn't notice or pay much attention to them.

Completing my 12 chapters from start to finish on retreat was an extremely satisfying moment. Many people expressed their amazement with how much I achieved in the short time on the writing retreat. Those who know the incredibly busy lifestyle I lead were most surprised that I was able to fit in the book writing process in between my teaching at school and the studio, and running my business.

Why did you decide to do the Ultimate 48 Hour Author Program for your first book?

Ever since I was a child I would write travel journals. When I moved to dance in Paris I wrote down my experiences every day, filling four journals that weighed 15kg! They were my most prized possessions. After I returned home, I wanted to share my experiences with others who were interested in the reality of living and working in Paris; sharing my highs and lows. I began to turn my diary notes into a book and then ... life got in the way. I got stuck in the overwhelming process of writing and compiling my notes, and *I had no idea what structure to follow*. I struggled to put aside time, and without any contacts in the book editing and publishing world, my book writing dreams were shelved.

Fast forward 10 years and I attended the Ultimate 48 Hour Author half-day workshop, curious about the concept. I was attracted to Natasa's enthusiasm and honesty, and was inspired to revisit my book publishing dreams. I have very limited free time to spare, certainly much less time than I had 10 years prior when I first attempted writing, and so the Ultimate 48 Hour Author program, *with quick turn around and unlimited support from numerous professionals from start to finish,* was extremely appealing to me.

I knew that I would finally be able to make my dream of writing a book a reality. I felt reassured knowing that there was support whenever I needed it, and was drawn to *the professional, personal approach.*

What is your best piece of advice you can share with a first-time author?

My best advice to share for first-time authors is to *back yourself!* I think the hardest part for me was finding the inner strength to believe in myself and my abilities so that I could actually see this project through to completion. Deciding on the purpose for writing the book helped me get started, and from there I continued to jot notes and ideas into my phone whenever they came to me.

What I initially wrote was not perfect, but once I'd made a start, the content began to flow and I was able to revisit my chapters during the editing process and fix things I wasn't happy with.

If you find yourself getting stuck, break things into smaller, more manageable tasks, and talk about your chapters with a mentor or friend. I had a two hour, one-on-one meeting and chapter unpack with Natasa that I recorded. Every time I got stuck, I would listen to our discussion again, and this would help me find my place and regain focus.

Often conversations with mentors and friends were what reminded me that I was able to make a difference and that I did have valuable content to share. You're never alone, but you have to back yourself before others will.

What has happened now that your first book is out?

The biggest change for me now that my book is released has been my *increased confidence* as an expert and leader. I now look at all my past challenges as opportunities to grow and share so that others can find success, and might not have to face these same difficulties.

I know that sharing my experiences and tips has positively helped other dancers, teachers, and studio owners, and this knowledge has inspired me to continue leading conversations and creating opportunities in my industry. My book has also given me a *point of difference for my business,* and consolidated my expertise in the dance sector, both locally and nationally.

Will you be writing more books in the future?
I am positive that I will write more books in the future, particularly now that I know the process of writing and publishing a book. Book writing is quite addictive! I would still like to share my memoirs from dancing at the Moulin Rouge. Also, in *Frou Frou to Fruition* I had to cut so many tips and ideas out to keep within a reasonable word limit so there's plenty more left to share there, too.

As my business continues to grow I learn new tricks, experiment with new ideas, and create exciting programs that I'm keen to share. I'd like to continue to positively influence dance teachers and studio owners, and assist them to build safe, healthy, creative spaces for the next generation of dancers.

To purchase Kym's book:
www.froufroutofruition.com

MONA ALHEBSI

Author of *Beat the Odds*

What is your book about and why did you write it?
Coming from a rural area in Ras Al Khaimah, a northern city in the United Arab Emirates, it is understood that the only accepted career for women would be the traditional one – being a wife and a mother.

In my book *Beat the Odds* I take the reader on a journey of the struggles I've been through, and how I have beaten the odds by rising to the challenge and choosing a different path to build a successful career in the hospitality industry. From there, I became highly educated and became an award-winning Emirati woman who paved the way for other UAE nationals to see working in hotels as a viable career option for a woman.

Beat the Odds is a reference and a guide to those who feel that they are stuck in their career and are unable to move forward to the next level. It is based on my real-life experiences, and it includes tried and tested methods that I've applied to achieve amazing results in career progression and industry exposure.

I wrote *Beat the Odds* because I could see through my career life that there was not a solid guide on this topic, and how much the majority of hoteliers tend to focus on the 'job', only to end up neglecting the 'career' aspect. This is detrimental to a person's personal and professional life.

The 11 focus areas covered in this book urge the reader to do things differently than the rest of their peers to rise and excel. Implementing these approaches, they can make the difference between being an average 'employee', and a thriving 'expert' in their field.

What was your biggest challenge in deciding to write your first book?
I was been thinking of writing a book for the past five years. Every time I thought about it I would be very excited in the beginning, however, the many saboteurs in my head pulled me back. Some of the concerns I used to have were: I don't know anyone in my circle/field/profession who has ever written a book, *most authors I know have their own business,* can I write a book while I'm still working, and how will my employer react? I also thought: writing a book is a complicated process, *I don't know from where to start,* do I really have the time to do this (I'm a working professional and hotel duty takes up most of my time), and maybe I need to *wait 'til I have more experience/money/time.*

These concerns and more kept rolling in my head until, luckily, I was introduced to the 48 Hour Author system.

Who were your biggest doubters and has their opinion changed now that you are published?
There will always be people who discourage us and doubt our abilities. On the contrary, there are others who cheer us on and want to see us succeed. The question is: which group do I choose to focus on most

of the time? Do I trust myself to do this? Can I foresee myself holding my book in my hand? How will I feel then? How many people's lives can be positively influenced by reading my book? These were my determining factors to write and publish my first book.

It was awkward for me when I started telling people about my intention of publishing a book. At that point, people's reactions reflected my own limiting beliefs, and how much I thought I can do it. Once I continued talking to more people about this exciting project, I started believing in myself, and my pitch started to sound different, and its impact on others changed accordingly.

I was very glad to see an increase in the number of supporters and people who were excited by this idea. My learning of this experience is no one will believe in you until you start believing in yourself and capabilities.

Why did you decide to do the Ultimate 48 Hour Author Program for your first book?

I attended Natasa's half-day seminar in Dubai last October because I had been thinking about publishing a book for some time. I was curious and wanted to know how someone can write a book in just 48 hours. I thought maybe they will have the answers for my questions, and can help me write the book that I have been dreaming of for so long.

After the seminar, I was 100% certain that I should go for it. I was the first to commit on the day. Ultimate 48 Hour Author is a unique program that has a very methodical system, and connections to all the relevant people who support you throughout the authoring process. Most importantly, they have helped many first-time authors already to publish their books. I'm glad I did, and I think Natasa and Moustafa had a big role to play in the publication of my first book. They are awesome!

What is your best piece of advice you can share with a first-time author?

Be clear on your intention as to why you have decided to write a book. For any good book to be published you need two key elements: the content, and the system. This is especially true for your first-time authoring experience. If you know what you are talking about, then you've got the content. The second part is following an effective system to make your publishing experience an enjoyable one, and ensure your message will get out in the right way to the right audience. In my case, that was with Ultimate 48 Hour Author.

Also remember, writing and publishing your book is only the beginning. In order to spread your message and continue your amazing journey to success, it's equally important to be associated with the right network of people before, during, and after publishing your book, so that you get the right comradery and continue to push your boundaries. As the popular saying goes: *If you want to go fast, go alone. If you want to go far, go together.*

What has happened now that your first book is out?

Amazing things started to happen when the news spread about my first book! I've always been highly educated, a top achiever, and an expert in my field, however, announcing to the world that I'm becoming a published author soon has **boosted my credibility, expanded my reach, and impacted people's perceptions about me positively.**

On a personal level, I feel more accomplished and fulfilled that my contributions are being valued, and I'm sharing my knowledge and expertise with other people who may be in desperate need to know that information to improve the quality of their life, and get closer to their goals.

I have also noticed a change in how my colleagues are approaching me, and an increase in the number of *speaking opportunities* that

I'm receiving from event organizers, and coaching requests that I receive from other professionals who ask for guidance on how to move their career to the next level.

Will you be writing more books in the future?
Definitely. I'm a writer at heart, and writing has always been an innate talent and my preferred tool to get my message across, change perspectives, and influence others. I've experienced most of my life rewarding triumphs after sending written pieces i.e. articles, emails, journals, etc., at different times and contexts.

I already have an idea about the topics that I'm going to publish, and how frequently I will be releasing content. Authoring with the help of Ultimate 48 Hour Author has been an extremely worthwhile experience, and I'm intending to do all my future books using this same system.

To purchase Mona's book:
www.monaalhebsi.com

PENNY NESBITT

Author of *Culture 101:*
Creating Places Where People Thrive and Profits Grow

What is your book about and why did you write it?

If the wealth of information from engagement and climate surveys is anything to go by, we have something of a problem on our hands when it comes to company culture. A $70 BILLION Australian dollars per year problem, according to a 2016 Gallup report on the cost of disengagement. That is a staggering amount of money by any standard, especially in a country

of just over 23 million people. And if, like many companies, you've got a lot of millennials working for you, they now make up the largest percentage of the workforce, and the largest percentage of the disengaged.

Running employee development programs over a couple of decades, my own experience is a microcosm of that sobering Gallup research. And it's what's inspired me to put pen to paper (fingers to laptop, actually).

In workshop after workshop, particularly when I'm running leadership programs for future or existing leaders, after a day or two of enthusiastic and engaged participation, after hearing, 'This is great stuff, makes so much sense, I'm learning a lot,' they ask, 'How come my leader doesn't do this/isn't doing this program? Why isn't our company doing this?'

To be honest, I'm usually stumped for an answer to that question. That's in situations where senior leaders (those who, in essence, drive the overall culture) have approved the development program, but don't seem to think it's necessary for them to attend a 'higher-ups' version of what's being rolled out, clarifying the part they play in walking the talk, thereby getting the best ROI (Return on Investment) on the program, and making sure any changes have the best chance of sticking. Bizarre, really, especially when you go back and look at those eye-watering figures on what disengagement and toxic cultures are costing.

Occasionally people share stories, either in the group or privately later, about a leader's behaviour that frankly falls into the category of 'truth is stranger than fiction' – some of these stories are seriously the stuff of a Hollywood writer's dreams.

Another disturbing fact: more heart attacks and sudden deaths amongst working people happen on a Monday than on any other day of the week, driven apparently by a massive surge of the stress hormones adrenaline and cortisol. Toxic cultures are basically killing people.

Inspired by these stories and by my own mind-numbing, soul-destroying experiences of toxic cultures, a couple of bosses from hell, and a confidence-draining redundancy or two, I decided it was time to do my bit in terms of making a difference by writing *Culture 101*.

What was your biggest challenge in deciding to write your first book?
I had **so much content**, and had done so much research that for a while I was **overwhelmed**! Trying to figure out what content and stories or anecdotes fitted under what chapter headings was a bit challenging, too, until I got into the swing of it.

Self-doubt was also a constant battle, with a little voice in the back of my head muttering away every now and then, 'Who'd want to read your book? There a lots more experienced/ qualified/smarter people than you.' After a while, as I pushed on, it got way easier to ignore the annoying little mutterer, which eventually disappeared altogether!

CULTURE 101

Creating places where people thrive and profits grow

PENNY NESBITT

Who were your biggest doubters and has their opinion changed now that you are published?

My doubters were varied and many! Seems most people thought my talk of writing a book was, at worst, hot air, at best, wishful thinking! The thrill of submitting the final manuscript for editing was absolutely exhilarating, and then a few weeks later, receiving the boxes of printed books – priceless! And *any doubt in anyone's mind was dispelled. People are in the main in awe that I actually wrote a book – doubters included!*

Why did you decide to do the Ultimate 48 Hour Author Program for your first book?

Like many people, I'd talked about and dreamed about writing a book for some time, but when I looked in to it I was overwhelmed by what was involved in getting it actually to the point of being printed! Having gone along to one of Natasa's 'taster' events, the impossible now felt possible, with Natasa and her team taking care of all the (many) confusing and detailed bits and pieces involved in the process of getting a book published – right down to author photos!

If I'd tried to do this on my own, a lot of time would have been wasted trying to find the right resources, at the right price, going down rabbit holes, and missing vital elements of the process, let alone finishing the writing. It meant I could concentrate on simply writing about my passion, and get the manuscript done!

What is your best piece of advice you can share with a first-time author?
People often hold back from any type of creative venture – painting, music, book writing – because someone else has already painted that scene, played that music, or written about that topic. I was stuck right there until I was given a great piece of advice: 'That's right, Pen, but YOU haven't written about this. This book is YOUR voice on culture.'

That single bit of advice freed me up to write from the heart, from the head, and from my own experience – no holds barred. The result? People tell me that reading the book is like having a chat with me, and is a real reflection of me as person, the authentic me on a page. It took courage, for sure, because once the book's out there, well, everyone knows your opinion and, of course, you can't please them all. My advice to these folks? Don't buy my book! I look forward to reading your book on the topic!

What has happened now that your first book is out?
I've had a couple of *book launches and was blown away by the numbers* of people who came out to support me. I've been *interviewed on 2UE*, and by *HR Daily*, have been invited to *MC a number of events, and ran two masterclasses at Convergence 2018* (a change management conference) that were so successful I've been asked to run the same classes again at another conference in August 2018.

I somehow managed to complete a Diploma of Positive Psychology and Wellbeing while finishing the book, which tied well as Culture 101 is steeped in research from the Positive Psychology movement. As a result a former boss contacted me, and I've been invited to take *aspects of Culture 101 into the education sector*, working to *create an online learning program aimed at teaching staff.*

The lesson here is with writing a book, it's not just a case of 'build (or write) it, and they will come.' *I've designed a new website, have really ramped up my social media presence, and am focused on face-to-face meetings, as well.*

Will you be writing more books in the future?
I've already started on a book called *Talks that Matter* which is the how-to aligned to the Four Keys to Culture that I talk about in *Culture 101* that forms the basis of a series of modular face-to-face 'culture hacks' such as Talks that Matters: Tough Talks; Talks that Matter: Strong Teams; Talks that Matter: You and Me (coaching).

And who knows, maybe I'll eventually get around to a work of fiction!

To purchase Penny's book:
www.pennynesbitt.com.au

RACHAEL SHELDRICK

Author of *Turbo Charged – How to Take Your Auto Repair Business from Survival to Success*

What is your book about and why did you write it?
Turbo Charged is the first book of its kind in Australia for auto repair business owners who know they need help to grow. I wrote the book for three reasons: to be able to easily help auto repair shop owners to become aware of the simply things they could do for their business to turn it around; to assist with credibility when being considered for speaking engagements; and I had a stand at a large industry expo 60 days after the retreat, and I wanted something the attendees could walk away with. A book was the perfect answer.

What was your biggest challenge in deciding to write your first book?
The biggest challenge was simply how to organise to get to Melbourne the following week for the retreat! I made a very quick decision to write the book once I knew Ultimate 48 Hour Author existed.

Who were your biggest doubters and has their opinion changed now that you are published?
My family were my biggest doubters, but once they saw the results of the published book they were excited for me.

Why did you decide to do the Ultimate 48 Hour Author Program for your first book?
I had a personal recommendation from a friend who knew Stuart and Natasa and vouched for their professionalism. After a 20-minute chat on the phone with Stuart I had no doubts whatsoever.

What is your best piece of advice you can share with a first-time author?
Just get it done!

Stop procrastinating!

What has happened now that your first book is out?

My book is on its **third print run**, and I have generated **more than $40,000 in book sales,** and contributed to **more than $750 000 worth of sales of my online programs and speaking fees.**

Will you be writing more books in the future?
I thoroughly enjoyed the process of becoming a published author using the Ultimate 48 Author system, but **rather than writing another book, I use the system to write new online programs for my clients** to be able to access and use to grow their businesses, no matter where they are in the world.

To purchase Rachael's book:
www.workshopwhisperer.com

SALLY THURLEY

Author of *She-Monk: Our Daily Life is the New Spiritual Practice*

What is your book about and why did you write it?

My book *She-Monk* came about through a calling to write, and a strong desire to free people from spiritual conditioning BS. I wanted to give people the tools that I knew worked, to overcome suffering, to heal by finding their reason for being, their soul's want, and learning how to become established enough in it to actually being it in the world. No more stress, anxiety, pushing, faking it. This is a path to happiness, inner peace, and self-realisation. It is the ultimate merging point of spiritual practice, and personal transformation.

After decades in an ashram and a lifelong love of spirituality then taking my attention to the world, I saw what matters and is practical, and what can make a difference. I call it being love on legs, living like the Dalai Lama, and having the best experience of the world. Yes, there is a way!

What was your biggest challenge in deciding to write your first book?

There were two things that got in the way of fulfilling this strong urge to write a book. Firstly, it was **which company to use**. I contacted many, but something never felt right; they were after numbers, and I wanted a personal, supportive 'for me' approach. Secondly, it was working out **how to get the book actually done** and not some project that will take years before it's finished. How will I know it's done, good enough? So, I sat on it for a few years. There was also confusion as to how to construct a chapter properly, how to have the right flow in the book.

Who were your biggest doubters and has their opinion changed now that you are published?
At the time, the **people closest to me were my biggest doubters,** subtly though. **My partner** at the time had a PhD and was also a published author of business books with a traditional publishing house. He was a perfectionist who doubted people less qualified than him could write a book. I had **some great friends who were threatened that I was moving ahead.** They wanted to write a book, as most people do, but never got past the talking about it stage. As I kept going, they started to make critical comments.

Why did you decide to do the Ultimate 48 Hour Author Program for your first book?
What I love about the Shakti or spiritual energy, about being open to faith and trusting the universe, is that everything works just as it should. I moved on. There are three spiritual approaches to everything: change the situation, change yourself/ perspective, or leave. If you take the ego and mind out of it and do what is right, everything works out. They have all bought my book and love it.

Things did get better when I was approached by a large and popular publishing house, then the naysayers took notice. As exciting as that was, the fine print was not attractive, and I would lose the freedom I wanted to write and use the book as I wanted to. Self-publishing was the way for me.

One day at the beginning of my new business, I decided to go to the city and start networking and meeting new people. I met this gorgeous lady who was telling me of the incredible work she does, and that she had just written a book. I couldn't believe it so asked her loads of questions. To my astonishment, she said she 'spoke' the book and did it in just 48 hours. What? That's like a dream come true, exactly what I wanted. I knew there had to be something unique and perfect out there for me, and this was it. She handed me a flyer for the Ultimate 48 Author Half-Day Workshop. I went straight home and booked in.

At the workshop I felt how genuine Natasa and Stuart are, and how passionate they are for us to get our books done and out there. I really liked how open they are and how intuitive, also. They are totally non-judgmental of anybody. I loved it. I signed up on the spot.

What is your best piece of advice you can share with a first-time author?
To all aspiring authors, I want you to know that the world needs your book, your business needs your book, so don't stop it happening due to being overwhelmed, confused, or overthinking. Get that book done! **Silence that inner critic**. Once you have become a published author, something **magic happens**. You have a **new confidence** and have opened the door to more books. Just do it. Have faith in the process and set your sights on how it will create fantastic opportunities for you. Come from a place of adding value to the world, that this book is your contribution to humanity, to society. Then it's not about you and the ego can't ruin your plans; you become immune to doubt and fear.

What has happened now that your first book is out?
Once *She-Monk* was released, **my brand started to take a new direction**. People began to see me, not only as the expert I am, but as someone who practices what she preaches. I started to be called the She-Monk, which has stuck, and had a tremendous

impact on my business. I will go to an event now where people do not know my name, but know I am the She-Monk. It's fabulous. It makes people so curious about me. *Eventually I worked out how to use the book in the way it was intended, to change people's lives and bring me an income.*

I turned She-Monk into the most amazing *12-month online interactive program* that is giving me everything I could have ever dreamed of, and I'm about to start offering six-month enrolments to keep the fun and transformation going. I am so happy. When you totally know what you do works and trust your knowledge and worth, have it all mapped out in a straightforward and easy-to-use book, you have everything you need to do well. Be prepared to think out of the box, and how you most want to leverage the book.

The most rewarding outcome is seeing the gorgeous people I work with drop their anxiety, their worries, their attachments to what keeps them stuck, and seeing them thriving and blooming in ways they never knew they could. I sense that is the same for the work Natasa and Stuart do with Ultimate 48 Hour Author. Total satisfaction.

Will you be writing more books in the future?
There are three more books in the pipeline, and all that is missing is the weekend away, being looked after, and being prompted to write, speak, them out, and get them done. Writing the first book and seeing how much content and knowledge I had set the way for these new companions that are ready to be birthed into the world. As I grow as a spiritual teacher, my books help me reach a wide audience and show my commitment to what I do, to others, and sets me apart from those who haven't got the same big vision for world healing and peace and an enlightened society.

To purchase Sally's book:
www.sallythurley.com/shemonk-book

WAEL IBRAHIM

Author of *Beat It!*

What is your book about and why did you write it?

My book deals with an issue that many people tend to skip and turn a blind eye to; it is a journey of recovery and empowerment over pornography addiction. It contains well-researched steps that can assist youngsters, as well as married couples, to get rid of their visual cocaine, known as pornography. The book was a response to the series of novels that were turned into movies with shades of darkness, greys, and

confusion. My book includes over 100 shades of hope, love, and sincere advice to those who have been screaming in silence looking for a solution to take them out of their misery.

The book has been planned for years, but the whole story began when I was approached by a young boy of 18 who was reflecting over committing suicide, and the reason for it was pornography. He had been struggling for years with his secret of watching pornography and masturbation, and could not tell or share his struggle with anyone. He revealed to me that he's been pleasuring himself to pornography for over seven years until he was diagnosed with erectile dysfunction. This was the main motive for me to research the topic, write about it, and try to find a solution to the thousands, if not millions of souls around the world.

What was your biggest challenge in deciding to write your first book?
The biggest challenge was **the amount of content** that I had, but could not put it together in a well-organized format. **I did not know where to start,** or how to tackle the issue in easy-to-understand and follow steps. Another issue that was also bothering me is the *nature of the topic itself;* how am I going to write on a very sensitive issue that is looked upon as taboo in many societies and cultures? But it was the advice of mentors, and dedicated team members of the Ultimate 48 Hour Author program who made my life easy, and a smooth journey of compiling the content into what is known now as the manual for breaking free from porn addiction.

Who were your biggest doubters and has their opinion changed now that you are published?
Doubters, or dream-breakers are everywhere. They were skeptical about the project. They called it a waste of time and money. In fact, some years ago I was dragged away from the stage while addressing the dangerous effects of pornography on the brain and relationships, where I was hoping to educate people and warn them from what pornography could lead them to. Others were trying to bury their heads in the sand, pretending that there was no problem. A few months after the book was out, those same people started inviting me to their circle and communities to conduct seminars and workshops on the same topic. They have finally realized that there is a demand and extreme need to help people, and raise awareness about this issue.

Why did you decide to do the Ultimate 48 Hour Author Program for your first book?
I wasn't planning to join the retreat organized by The Ultimate 48 Hour Author AT ALL. I thought it wasn't really for me. I attended the half-day workshop, and I really enjoyed plenty of tips that were presented, but joining the program was a bit of a challenge. I recall

a participant during the workshop asking me, 'Do you see yourself attending the retreat?' My response was, 'Absolutely not.'

FIFTY - PLUS SHADES OF HOPE

Wael Ibrahim

That wasn't because there was no value offered; in fact, the half-day workshop was full of gems and tricks that already could help in a great way. It was the doubts that I could get all this content organised, planned, and spoken/recorded in just 48 hours! When I got on the phone that same night with Natasa, I was convinced that this is what I wanted to pursue. It was her professionalism and confidence that brought me on that beautiful journey, but above all, the sincere and genuine words of advice she gave me over that same phone call that made me realize that it was time to let someone else lead my passion and bring it into light.

What is your best piece of advice you can share with a first-time author?

I would like to use the same words of advice given by Natasa during the retreat. It is seven words that changed my mindset forever: *'Say yes, and then work out how.'*

'No fear no more' has been my slogan until now. Even as I am writing this, I am thinking to myself, 'There are so many people who could write much better than myself, but I don't care because they are not ME. Plus, Natasa is there for me – she's going to edit, and make me sound smarter.'

In short, don't let your fear eat up your life and the things that you can benefit people with. You have got something to offer to this world, and you are the expert, so let it out and the rest will be very easy.

What has happened now that your first book is out?
A lot has happened. I've been invited to so many radio shows around the world, namely Malaysia, South Africa, as well as Sydney. I've been invited to so many *'train the trainers'* programs to raise awareness about the dangerous effect of pornography, and how to offer the necessary treatment to those who are addicted to it. I've been invited to **seminars and conferences to speak about the subject,** and people now are considering me to be one of the experts in the field. *Last conference I spoke at in the Philippines was attended by over 10,000 people.* Enough said.

Will you be writing more books in the future?
Oh yeah. Already writing two motivational books at the moment, and three other books idea are on my to-do list.

To purchase Wael's book:
www.amazon.com/-/e/B0199MH5K2

ABOUT THE AUTHOR

Natasa Denman was born and raised in Skopje, Macedonia. At age 14 she emigrated to Melbourne, Australia to be with her mum, after being separated for two and a half years. She didn't speak English, and initially found it challenging to fit into the new country and culture. Her zest for learning and achievement fast-tracked this process, and she had high performance results in her academic endeavors.

Natasa has a Bachelor of Applied Science (Psychology/Psycho-physiology), a Diploma in Life Coaching, is a NLP Practitioner Certification, a Practitioner of Matrix Therapies, holds a Black Belt in Taekwondo, and is a Professional Certified Coach (PCC) through the International Coaching Federation.

Being creative and writing books is something she never planned to do. Her passion for business and marketing was the reason she wrote her first book *The 7 Ultimate Secrets to Weight Loss* in June 2011. This book put her first business on the map, and enabled her husband to join her full-time in the business a year later.

She also wrote *Ultimate 48 Hour Author, Natasa Denman Reveals ..., 1000 Days to a Million Dollar Coaching Business from Home*, is a contributor to *You Can ... Live the Life of Your Dreams*, and *Speaking Successfully*. She is a co-author of *Ninja Couch Marketing, Bums on Seats, and Guilt Free Parents*.

Ultimate 48 Hour Author came about as a result of the success books have brought to Natasa's business. Aside from books,

she has also written five programs, and has three licensed systems that are being utilised by others internationally in their businesses.

She is now known as the Ultimate 48 Hour Author. Natasa is a highly sought after professional speaker (CSP accredited), and Australia's leading authority on helping first-time authors publish their books. She has helped more than 250 solopreneurs become first-time published authors in just four years in Australia, USA, New Zealand, and UAE. She also has clients from 10 other international countries.

In eight short years in business, Natasa has been nominated for The Telstra Businesswoman of the Year twice, and was a finalist in AusMumpreneur of the Year in Product Innovation.

Appearing in all major media outlets across Australia including the *Sydney Morning Herald*, the *Financial Review*, and the *Age*, Natasa is changing the way people do business in Australia, and the world.

She now runs a 7-figure business with her husband and three children, traveling the world spreading her message and helping small businesses thrive. This year, Natasa's mum also joined the business.

The Denman Family's passion is to continue to build this as a fully-fledged family business, helping thousands around the world become first-time authors without compromising on also living a balanced lifestyle. Their motto is *Work Hard – Play Hard*, whereby they work intensely for five and half months in the year, spend 2.5 months building new systems and value to what they do, and they travel and holiday four months of the year.

This is what they want to enable others to create when building their own entrepreneurial ventures with the help of a published book.

Ultimate 48 Hour Author lives by four values: Fun, Fast, Fame, and above all, FAMILY.

Natasa's websites:
www.natasadenman.com
www.writeabook.com.au

Email: natasa@natasadenman.com

EXPLORE

- Want to discover if you should write a book this year?
- Unsure on how to put the pieces of the puzzle together?

If you are ready to begin your author journey but are still on the fence if it is worth your time and effort, here is the best place to start.

1. Join our amazing **Author Your Way to Riches** Facebook group and be a part of a community of thousands of others that are on the same journey as you. Ask questions, learn from their experiences, and arm yourself with all the information you need to help you decide your next steps.

AUTHOR YOUR WAY TO RICHES - FACEBOOK GROUP

YOUR
BOOK?

https://tinyurl.com/authoryourwaytoriches

2. Join our Ultimate 48 Hour Author Academy for **FREE**. Access trainings and enjoy exclusive member only access to the hottest resources we have available to help you overcome your procrastination and self-doubt.

THE ULTIMATE 48 HOUR
AUTHOR ACADEMY

https://ultimate48hourauthor.teachable.com

ACCELERATE

Writing a book is important to you – and so should making an impact with it be! You don't want to be one of those people with a garage full of books. You don't want to be the best kept secret.

You want to get your book out there. To build your profile, credibility, and leverage your book to its full potential.

Here is your chance to LEVEL UP.

1. Attend our game-changing **Blueprint for Book Writing Success Seminar.** Attended by thousands of people from more than 15 countries, this live and interactive seminar teaches the exact blueprint to write, publish and leverage your first book.

REGULAR LIVE SEMINARS FOR AUSTRALIA and USA/CANADA TIME ZONES, BOOK YOUR SPOT HERE:
https://writeabook.com.au/writing-workshops/

2. The Proven Book Writing Success Formula. **Our Ultimate Book Planner** is your first-class ticket to your book's completion. With all the templates, systems, and mentoring at your fingertips, gone is the confusion and disorganisation that plagues most first-time authors. With this planner, it is time to make your book a reality!

ENTER CODE **ACCELERATE** to RECEIVE $10 OFF at CHECKOUT
https://writeabook.com.au/shop/

DOMINATE

Already done much of the hard work and ready to share your message on a global scale?

1. If you are ready to self-publish, Ultimate World Publishing is your best option. With a dedicated publications manager and world-class editors, design, and layout teams, your book will be bookstore quality and reflect your personality and brand. With Ultimate World Publishing, 'It is Your Book, Your Way'.

BOOK A CHAT WITH OUR PUBLISHING TEAM
https://writeabook.com.au/ultimate-world-publishing/

2. The pinnacle of our **Ultimate 48 Hour Author** experience is our **3-Day Virtual Retreat**. By application only, this bespoke experience is the guaranteed way to become the published author you want to be. More than 500 people can't be wrong!

It is an experience like no other and combines industry leading:

- Education
- Masterminding
- Mentoring
- Writing blocks, and of course
- A whole lot of fun along the way!

TO SEE IF THE RETREAT IS RIGHT FOR YOU –
BOOK A CHAT TODAY
https://tinyurl.com/authorqualifyingchat

NOTES

CPSIA information can be obtained
at www.ICGtesting.com
Printed in the USA
BVHW031227140422
634332BV00004B/136